A Guide to Apartment House Management

A Training Manual for Apartment House Managers

by
M. M. "Steemy" Holt

authorHOUSE™

1663 LIBERTY DRIVE, SUITE 200
BLOOMINGTON, INDIANA 47403
(800) 839-8640
WWW.AUTHORHOUSE.COM

First published by AuthorHouse 09/26/05

ISBN: 1-4208-1830-9 (sc)

Printed in the United States of America
Bloomington, Indiana

This book is printed on acid-free paper.

Second Edition

Contents

Introduction

This book is written for people who are thinking about going into resident managership. It is also for those many hard working, underpaid, and sometimes mistreated peple who are already in the field.

Some background information about property management itself will be useful. Around the early 1990's many people had invested in rental property. They lived in it, and managed it themselves in order to have retirement incomes or to supplement their present incomes. Just after World War I, there was an inflationary spiral in the economy of the nation, and these owners found themselves with much larger incomes than they had dreamed of. Wanting to travel or otherwise live a more leisurely life, they turned rather naturally to their favorite real estate agents or brokers and asked for their help in taking care of their property, collecting the rents and depositing the proceeds. The agents or brokers received a certain compensation for this service, usually in the form of a percentage of the gross income. They soon found that to handle this property was very much to their advantage as it gave them both a ready source of property to sell and exchange and a ready source of customers who might want to buy other property. This was in addition to the income made on the actual work of managing.

So the management company was born; and traditionally it has been involved with the real estate industry. Through the years it has undergone development, and some laws and regulations have been placed on it, but the situation remains that anyone who has the knowledge and experience to manage property can feasibly become a property manager, if he can sell himself to the property owner as a person who can do the job.

CHAPTER 1

TYPES OF MANAGEMENT

There are many kinds of people you will come in contact with when you start looking for a position as a resident manager of an apartment house. There are also many different kinds of management companies.

SINGLE OWNERSHIP

Probably the most pleasant and agreeable way to work as a resident manager is to be responsible directly to the owner of the property. Most single owners do not want to live in their property, personally attend to maintenance, renting and rent collection, and have their lives constantly interrupted by business, as you people who hire yourselves out as resident managers must do. A good many single owners of several buildings will, however, themselves handle the bookwork, bills, mortgages and insurance coverage, and will inspect their properties and see to needed maintenance.

GROUP OWNERSHIP

Within the large and expanding industry of apartment-house construction, many people have banded together in groups of five, ten, or more for the purpose of buying a large complex. Such a group will then either hire a management company to manage the property or decide to manage it themselves. Unless this group of owners has set up a system of control among themselves, working with them can become a frustrating and nerve-wracking experience for the person whom they hire to live on and manage the property. They should have one and only one spokesman to whom the resident manager is responsible and all their different ideas should be discussed in meetings; otherwise the resident manager will be plagued with conflicting orders as to how his job is to be done. One manager became so annoyed with this sort of operation that he burst in upon an investors' meeting and demanded that one spokesman be appointed, or else he would resign. He received his release a week later, which was unfair, as he was only asking for that which he was entitled to in the first place.

SAVINGS AND LOAN COMPANIES AND BANKS

Savings and loan companies, banks and other lending institutions that finance the building of apartment houses will not normally own and manage this property. But in a declining market, when the supply of living quarters greatly exceeds the demand for them, many investors find that the income on their property is not even paying the mortgage. The lending institutions are then forced to repossess the property; and they will set up departments within their companies to manage the repossessed buildings until such time as they can be resold, and will hire property managers who have the knowledge, experience, and background for this work. Such a department will then operate much like the property management company, which will be discussed later. You who are planning to be a resident manager in this setup will be making your application to one of these men hired as property managers, or to one of his employees, and your contact and communication will be the same as in working with a management company.

INVESTMENT COMPANIES

An investment company is somewhat the same as a number of investors who band together to buy property. The difference Is that instead of the group being partners in a particular project, the investment company is formed by a group of people, small or large, for the general purpose of buying and operating income properties. The properties are bought in the name of the company, instead of in the names of individuals. In this way the company can invite investment by the public and thus secure additional monies with which to buy more property. Investors not only get shares in the company but can look forward to an income return on their invested capital.

These companies are sometimes small, with eight to twenty-five buildings that may have a variety of uses. On the other hand, some of them are very large indeed, stretching across the nation. The companies, whatever their size, set up property management departments that do all the manual labor of seeing that the property is properly cared for. In the small company there may be only one property manager, in the large company there may be numerous property managers, with supervisors over supervisors, up to the top. The prospective resident manager will be making his application to the property manager or one of the property managers, or to one of his employees. The resident manager of an individual building will be responsible to the property manager who hired him, and his contact and communication with the company will be through him.

MANAGEMENT COMPANIES WITHIN REAL ESTATE FIRMS

Many real estate firms have found that their property management departments can be much more valuable to them than just for the prospect lists and the income from managed properties. Such a firm has a management department all ready to use when it takes property in on trade, so to speak. The firm advances the money for a down payment on a piece of property in order to allow a buyer to purchase a larger or better property. The real estate firm is limited by law in how long it can hold this property before consummating the sale. Hopefully it will sell this property on which it has made a down payment, within the limit set by law and be able then to transfer title from the previous owner directly to the new owner. During this time, the property must be cared for, and to do this job, the real-estate firm has a ready-made management department.

The firm will hire a qualified person to be the property manager, and he may or may not have assistant property managers under him, depending on the number of buildings involved. The property manager, his assistant or one of his employees, will be the resident manager's contact and communication with the firm.

PROPERTY MANAGEMENT COMPANIES

Still another kind of company the prospective resident manager will come in contact with is the property management company, which is organized for the single and primary purpose of managing other people's property. Such companies ordinarily do not own, or have a vested interest in, any of the properties they manage. They actively solicit owners or groups of owners and convince them that they can do a better job of managing their property than someone else. They manage properties on a percentage of the gross income. They will have a staff of property managers, assistant property managers and other employees, to do all the jobs that need doing, commensurate with the number of buildings they manage. The property managers will be the contacts for the resident managers.

The foregoing gives you some idea of the various kinds of organizations with which the prospective resident manager may be working. It is not necessary to know the names of the owners of a building to be a good resident manager, and sometimes it is better if you don't. If your particular company is doing its job well and working in close contact with the investors and owners, you, as a resident manager, probably will never come in contact with an owner or investor.

With the inflationary spiral of the past decade, investment companies, their property management departments, and property management companies have grown and multiplied with head-spinning rapidity. Unfortunately, along with all this rapid growth, there have been hired a number of people as managers of investment companies and as property managers who have neither the background nor the experience, let alone the knowledge, to do their job. Many of them have no aptitude for public or employee relations. The attitude of some of these people is to hire without interviews, fire without cause and never give time or guidance to the resident manager. New resident managers have been moved into buildings without the previous managers having been given notice until the last minute. The compensation in lieu of notice has been inadequate or nil. Couples have taken jobs in complexes at very unfair wages. One couple was known to have been managing a 70-unit complex for rent and $75 a month. Another couple was managing a 30-unit building, with swimming pool, sauna, and many hallways to keep clean, for rent and $50 a month, and when they took the building it was two-thirds empty and they filled it up. There is another couple managing a 200-unit building for rent and $600 a month. A 200-unit building is a full-time job for both husband and wife; if they were to take just ordinary, separate jobs in today's market, they would make much more between them.

Resident managers have been known to be hired on the telephone, only to be fired in a few months, without cause, notice or compensation. After being hired they are given very little time, a lot less training and guidance, little instruction and no communication. The attitude seems to be, "If they don't work out, get a new manager." Consequently, resident managers make a lot of changes, and soon, after trying several companies, they become unhappy with the entire industry, feeling that no one is to be trusted.

Policy in a company* is made at the top and filters down to the very least on the payroll. It can be seen in talking with any person in the company, because it shows at every level.

*The word "company" will hereafter refer to any type of ownership or managership of an apartment house, whether it is a single owner, a group of owners, an investment company, or a managing company.

Nothing can replace honesty and forthrightness in good business relations. A resident manager and his property manager should have a free flow of communication between them, and the resident manager should be given time, instruction, guidance and patience so he can learn to do his job properly. The resident manager is the grassroots of the industry, the man on the firing line who either makes it or breaks it for the investors. While he is the most underpaid, mistreated and ignored man in the firm, it is in his hands that the management company and investors have placed their faith. He is the man who rents the apartments and keeps the tenants happy, and he should be treated with respect and compensated accordingly.

You, as a resident manager, can help to upgrade the industry by insisting on a proper interview, knowing how much you are to be paid, not accepting less than the job is worth, and demanding that you have proper on-the-job training and good communication with the company. If your company does not use a written contract with resident managers, try at least to extract a promise that if you are released from your job, you will be given proper notice and compensation. Also, promise yourself that if you have been given proper notice, you will stay on the job and do it to the best of your ability until the company can install a new manager.

If it is your misfortune to come upon one of those misguided persons who cannot be bothered to give you the time of day, let alone a little of himself, quit! Go and find another company. There are a lot of good ones, with good people in them. People work for people, not money. Never forget that!

There exists an official designation of degree of proficiency in property management. It is the C.P.M. – Certified Property Manager – awarded by the Institute of Real Estate Management. A person is granted this designation only after long years of experience and study. He must also pass certain examinations given by the institute and must subscribe to certain regulations and codes of ethics. This man will know his job well and be keenly aware of his responsibilities to his employees, tenants and investors.

CHAPTER II

JOBS AVAILABLE TO RESIDENT MANAGER

WHAT IS A PROPERTY MANAGER?

The job of property manager is *not* one of the jobs available to you as a resident manager. Still, you definitely should know just what his job is.

"The" property manager may be the single owner with whom you work directly. He may be the person you are directly responsible to who has been chosen from a group of persons who own your building. He may be the manager and property manager of an investment firm, or the property manager hired by the manager of the investment firm. He may be an assistant to the property manager in a large firm, or he may be an employee of a savings and loan company that has repossessed a building. In any case, there will be one person you are directly responsible to, and that person will be a "property manager." In large complexes just finishing construction and working toward getting the apartments filled for the first time, this person is sometimes called the "project manager."

The property manager is either the person who sets policy as owner or one of a group of owners, or the person who establishes policy for a company, through a comprehensive knowledge of the company's policy or through discussions with the investors. Policies will vary widely from company to company and owner to owner.

Your property manager should have been chosen for his sound background, experience and general knowledge in the rental and maintenance business as a whole. He will be called upon to make many quick decisions and usually must be available twenty-four hours a day, in case of emergencies. He will make recommendations to the company on advertising to build more traffic and on insurance, in detail. He will make projections of future business. He will hire resident managers and train them. He will hire maintenance crews to do the larger jobs, sometimes deal with unions, sometimes be implicated in lawsuits. He will discuss and recommend whether or not to install some new facility.

The property manager is responsible for keeping records of vacancies, leases, rental agreements, maintenance costs, what each building needs, what it will cost, which units need repairs or paint and which units have been repaired or painted. This information must be available to the company at all times and must be kept up to date. The property manager will do the inspection of your building himself or will hire an assistant to do part of his job, or he may want his resident managers to do a good bit of the inspection and report needed repairs and maintenance.

The property manager is responsible for the collection of rents. Some companies mail out statements to tenants and normally collect rent by mail, but there are always some tenants who will make their rent payments in person to the resident manager. Other companies prefer that all rent be paid to the resident manager and then the property manager is responsible for seeing that the rent money is collected from the resident manager and deposited. Some companies you may work with will require that the resident manager make deposits daily in a local bank, and you will be required to keep some small accounts for your company, to be reported to your property manager.

Your property manager is responsible for periodic inspection of your building. He may call on you once a week, once a month or once every two or three months, depending on company policy. He will want to check your vacant units, check your cleaning methods, see if your grounds are properly maintained, and see if your public spaces are clean, orderly, and not in need of some repair. He might just walk around the grounds on one call and crawl up on the roof on another call. It is his job to know each and every building on his list, from top to bottom, and keep an eye to its repair. It is his job to know everything about your job – to check on you and help you to do your best for the company. When the property manager calls on you, he should always take time to sit and talk with you about any problems you have run into during his absence or that you have previously reported to him.

Needless to say, the property manager is a very busy man, traveling his areas endlessly and putting in long hours. The resident manager should always be aware of the pressures on his property manager and not waste his time.

RESIDENT MANAGER OF 70 UNITS AND UP

The resident manager of a building of 70 units and up will need some assistance. From 70 to perhaps 125 units, he may or may not have an assistant manager who lives on the premises. This will depend on how much maintenance is done by outside people called in to help. The manager and his wife will work as a team, dividing the work between them as they see fit.

In the larger units, it is generally a full-time job for both husband and wife. Usually the man is primarily responsible for the rental of vacant apartments, looks into tenants requests, inspects apartments and oversees those hired to do work in the complex. He is responsible for collecting rent and getting it to its proper destination and for obtaining rents that are past due. His wife keeps the records and makes the reports to the central office, keeps the building office open when the man is out, and oversees the cleaning of vacant units. The resident manager of a large complex is responsible for the hiring of his assistant managers, or should be; at the least he should have the authority to interview them, and pass judgment on them, before they are hired.

ASSISTANT RESIDENT MANAGER

Apartment complexes of 70 to 100 units may or may not have an assistant resident manager – either a maintenance man or a couple, depending on the size of the building, the maintenance needed and how much extra help the company hires to get all the jobs done. Apartment complexes of over 125 units should have an assistant management couple who also live on the premises. This lets both couples have much-needed time off. The hours and work are divided by agreement between the two, with the manager, of course, being the superior. The assistant manager is usually a man talented in doing all the handy-man types of jobs. He will be called upon to do all the minor maintenance, take care of swimming pools, oversee the cleaning of public areas, and grounds, and often do painting and carpentry. His wife will clean the vacated apartments, or oversee the cleaning, and the two of them, together or separately, will spell the manager and his wife for their days off. While they are working as assistants, they should be learning the job of the manager, for one day they will want to try for a full managership.

Days off for assistant manager and resident manager will be one to two a week, depending on company policy. The assistant manager will most generally be the one called on after hours. If a repair is for emergency maintenance, he will call the resident manager, and together they will decide how urgent the matter is.

An apartment building of 70 to 100 units may very well get along with a full-time maintenance man, who may or may not live on the premises, and his wife will be free to take outside work and may be able to spell the manager and his wife evenings by taking after-hours calls.

RESIDENT MANAGER OF 50 TO 70 UNITS

Buildings of 50 to 70 units generally do not require the full time of both man and woman of a couple. This again depends on company policy. Some companies will make it a full-time job for both parties by having the man do all the minor maintenance, exterior cleaning and interior painting, and will pay them a livable salary. Most of the time the wife will do the renting, record keeping and cleaning, including the public spaces. The husband will care for the lawns, walks, drives, light bulbs, etc., evenings and week ends, but during the week he will be employed in anther job. If there is an unusual amount of work out of doors, the company will hire it done by outside labor or a traveling gardener.

RESIDENT MANAGER OF 30 TO 50 UNITS

Buildings of 30 to 50 units will almost never need the full time work of both husband and wife. Usually the wife stays at home, rents vacant apartments, take tenant requests, checks out problems between tenants, collects rent and sees that it is deposited or picked up by the property manager. She is responsible for cleaning the vacated apartments and getting them ready for rental, keeping the laundry rooms, hallways, stairs, walks and decks clean, and will list those things she is unable to do, so her husband can do them evenings and week-ends. The husband will take care of the grounds, swimming pool, if any, and do any minor repair he is capable of, evenings or week ends, or whenever else he is not at his regular job. Conceivably the situation could be reversed for older couples when the husband is on Social Security and the wife is still of working age and wishes to continue. In buildings of this size, the resident manager may or may not be called on to do spot painting, carpet shampooing and more than minor maintenance, depending again on company policy. If there is an undue amount of exterior work to be done, such as large grass areas or much gardening, the company will usually hire some or all of the work done by outside labor. It then becomes the resident manager's responsibility to see that such work is done properly.

RESIDENT MANAGER OF UNDER 30 UNITS

Apartment buildings of 30 or fewer units may or may not be much the same for a resident manager as the larger buildings of 30 to 50 units. It stands to reason that the smaller the building, the less work there is to do.

In the very much smaller buildings, however, the resident manager is much more likely to be working directly with an owner, and here he would do anything that the owner asked him to do, and they would agree on the wage and rent together. In a building of, say 12 to 15 units, the manager may be called on to do everything, just as if the building were his own. On the other hand, he may only be required to rent vacant apartments, collect rent, and see that it gets to the owner intact.

There will be much diversity in operating methods among various-sized apartment houses. A person who aspires to be a resident manager should be aware of this, and make himself able to fill the job required by any company.

RENTAL AGENT

In very large complexes with one section just finished, the construction company, or its agent, will place a person on duty in the office during regular office hours to show prospective tenants and other lookers the model units, give out brochures, show projection sketches of the completed complex and do anything else that might sell people on later moving into the yet unfinished apartment units. This person is called a rental agent and often is a woman. She is paid a salary and may or may not live on the premises. Her primary duties are to rent apartments and to seek reservations for unfinished apartments.

When the apartment complex has been completed, she will be replaced with a resident manager.

Another who might be called a rental agent is the person who keeps regular hours in the office of an established apartment complex. She generally lives on the premises, takes phone calls, accepts rent that is paid at the office and makes deposits. She is the one who shows the apartments for rent. Maintenance is taken care of by personnel hired by the company and she directs them to needed repairs. This job more often than not is filled by a woman, and her husband has little or nothing to do with it.

CHAPTER III

ARE YOU BEING PAID ADEQUATELY?

Although the newspaper ads ask for couples to manage apartment houses, the resident manager's job is primarily the woman's job in buildings of up to 70 units. In such buildings the compensation is likely to be such that the man of the house must have an outside job in order to make a living. It could be the other way around – the man staying home and taking care of the apartment house and the woman filling an outside job; or it could be that a retired couple take a small complex in order to supplement their income, yet not jeopardize their Social Security income. Compensation usually includes the rent you would pay if you were not resident manager and also the utilities. This money is not reported as income and so is tax-free.

UNDER 70 UNITS

To know whether you are being adequately paid for your labors, you must know something of the way salaries are reached for various complexes. Some are set by a percentage of the gross income of the complex. For example: A building has 40 units. Some rent for $350 a month and others for

$250. There is a possible gross income of $12,000 a month. If you receive 5 percent of the gross, your total income will be $600 a month – your rent of, say $250 will be deducted and the remainder paid to you in cash – if your building is full and grossing its full potential.

If there is a declining market and your building loses tenants and is grossing only part of its full potential, your income will come down accordingly.

A much fairer method of setting salaries for resident managers is by the number of units in the complexes. This can cover a wide range, from $10 to $20 a unit. Ten dollars is on the low side, $20 on the high side. If we use the same apartment house of 40 units and set the unit rate of $15, the gross income for the resident manager will be $600 a month, from which your own rent will be deducted, with the balance paid in cash. In a declining market with high vacancy factors your compensation will not vary.

Actually, when there is a high vacancy factor, your workload as resident manager will be heavier. When an apartment is vacated, the company must then do any needed maintenance, such as carpet shampooing, painting, drapery cleaning, and repairing. The vacated apartment must be cleaned immediately to determine what part of the former tenant's security deposit is to be refunded; then, if it needs painting and other repair, there will be more cleaning up after the painters and repairmen have finished. There will be the weekly care of the empty apartments, and you will feel yourselves much more confined to the building so as not to miss a possible rental. Therefore, whether there is high occupancy or low occupancy, your income should be stable - something you can depend on.

In most complexes of under 50 units, the woman of the team is required to clean vacated apartments. For this she should be paid an hourly wage in addition to the base salary, which wage comes out of the vacating tenant's deposits that were made when they moved in. Few tenants leave their apartments in such good condition that the resident manager is not required to do some cleaning, although there are some that come pretty close. The deposit made by the tenant is for the purpose of covering any damage to the apartment and the cost of any cleaning required. Normal wear and tear to the apartment should not be deducted for. If you are not being paid for cleaning vacated apartments or are being paid a flat rate, then you are being treated unfairly by your employer. Any such unfair treatment or any undue delay in refunding deposits only creates frustration for the resident manager and ill will for the managing company.

Another way to figure out whether you are being paid properly is to keep track of the actual hours you spend in managing your building. This does not mean the hours you may spend sitting in your apartment waiting for prospective tenants or visiting tenants or sleeping. Keep a record of the hours that husband and wife spend doing something for the apartment building. If your hourly wage is less than minimum wage, then you are not being paid enough.

OVER 70 UNITS

In the larger complexes, you will find, the rate per unit goes down, or it will be split in order to hire a maintenance man, or a second couple as assistant managers. A resident manager for a 200-unit complex may find a few jobs that will pay, $900 or $1,000 a month plus rent, but more likely the salary will be $700 to $800 a month plus rent. Bear in mind that it takes two employees, working full time, often with only one day a week off, to earn this much money. This is not considered high income, though it is a livable income. It might be that the property manager has figured the 200-unit building at the rate of $6 a unit. This would mean that a resident manager could earn a gross income of $1,200 a month. However, he would then have to hire someone to do maintenance, clean apartments, etc. It would cost him more than a dollar a unit to hire the extra help needed, so he decides to split the $1,200 and hire an assistant couple to do the work that he cannot possibly handle alone. Thus the property manager, and the company are hiring four people to work for them at $1,200 a month. This certainly is not much pay for the work that a resident manager and an assistant resident manager have to do. But property managers and companies are going to continue underpaying their resident managers as long as there are people who will sell themselves so cheap, or until they find that by paying better wages, they can get better-trained, more outgoing, harder-working people who in the long run will make more money for them.

It is up to you who are already managing and you who aspire to manage to inform yourselves thoroughly on every aspect of the resident manager's duties. To the beginner: start at the bottom, with a small building. Learn every phase of it, then try for a little larger building. Don't take on a huge complex with all its problems on the second or third try. It will take three to five years to work up to that, and you should get all the prior experience you can in easy stages.

Young people still in school can start in this way and supplement their income with just the rent for a while. If you plan to live in apartment houses for a number of years, there is no reason why you should not attempt this type of work for that "second job," in order that the wife may stay at home instead of "working out." There are many advantages to being a resident manager. The work is varied, you meet many pleasant and interesting people and can make lifelong friendships. Many couples will drop out of the work for a while, raise a family, and buy a home for the children, then go back to it in later years, when the children are grown and to maintain a home is no longer desired. To the retired couple it can provide just what is needed to keep them from being a burden on their children and to give them a feeling of still being useful in a world they might otherwise feel has discarded them for being too old.

Being a resident manager is a confining job. You must be ready to meet the public at nine in the morning and usually be on call until nine in the evening. You can never leave your building unattended. You will more than likely be underpaid. With all this, it still can be a gratifying job, pleasant and full. You will make lasting friendships and feel needed. If you are truly a good manager, you will get rich but not with the dollar, you will get tired but not from boredom, and you will be a better person for it.

CHAPTER IV

COMPANY POLICY

The word "policy" has been used in so many different ways that one is often at a loss to know its true meaning. What is the policy concerning pets? The policy concerning tenants, employees, hiring, firing, cleaning, renting, etc.? To most of us the word "policy" suggests rules and regulations more than it does the character of the company that brought about the rules and regulations.

The dictionary tells us that "policy" is prudence or sagacity in the conduct of affairs; a course of plan of administrative action; a system of management based on self-interest as opposed to equity. The prudent person looks at his actions of today in light of how they will affect tomorrow. He is careful to avoid errors in following the most politic and profitable course; he is cautious and worldly-wise. The sagacious person is rational, clear-sighted, discerning. He can often see in slight indications, by instinct or intuition, that which may be from others hidden. "Sagacious" is not the same as "shrewd," which often carries with it the idea of trickery. Nor is it the same as "wise," which often means profound. Sagacity deals with practical matters. Self-interest refers to a business's primary purpose of making money on its investment, while equity deals more with justice and relates more to courts. This is not to say that companies motivated by self-interest must not concern themselves with fair and "equitable" treatment of their employees and tenants.

Therefore, company policy is not rules and regulations, nor method of organization, but the reasonable and farsighted thinking that brought about the making of those rules and regulations.

When a resident manager is working for a company that handles many buildings, he should feel assured that the company is run by people who have used foresight and intelligence in putting together the organization and in setting up all its rules and regulations – people who have used prudence and sagacity in their dealings with other human beings.

RULES AND REGULATIONS

When four or five hundred men, women and children – and perhaps some animals – live on three to ten acres, as in a 200- to 250-unit complex, the area becomes a congested one. The tenants will share common swimming pools, laundry rooms, parking area, game and exercise rooms, etc. It is easy to see that if there were no rules or regulations about the use of this space by the people occupying it, the area would soon become a slum with each person contributing his share to making it that. Soon discriminating and thougthful people would refuse to live there, the property would deteriorate, the company would not make any money and the property would have to be sold at a sacrifice.

All these people have television sets, radios, stereos and automobiles. Some may have pets and children. A good many people are considerate and concerned with the welfare of those around them, but many others are not, so rules and regulations must be set up for the observance and benefit of all who live in such an area. The rules cannot favor one or another, but must be for all, including the resident manager. For example, if you hope to manage a building without pets, you must be without a pet yourself.

TRAINING

Your company should be continually training you as a resident manager. This is not to say you should always be going to a school, or that it takes months and years to learn how to use and fill out the many forms involved. Rather, there should be regular and frequent communication between you and your company. Each day problems will arise that are just a little different from any you have faced before. The resident manager should keep a faithful record of all problems and questions and discuss them with his property manager on his regular visit. The company should plan meetings with other resident managers, so that different circumstances can be discussed with others who are having similar problems. A large company, with many apartment houses, should have some kind of newsletter that is sent to the resident managers regularly, with news of the company and other managers, so that you feel like a member of a family. Training schools are fine for the inexperienced but are boring to the veteran managers who long for associations with their own kind to discuss their buildings and people.

The monthly or bimonthly meeting of resident managers could always be programmed to bring interesting and worthwhile information to the group. All of this is under the head of training, since training is learning – and none of us is too old to learn.

PETS

Dogs, cats, hamsters, gerbils, skunks, monkeys, canaries, parakeets and lizards are all pets. Most resident managers will be dealing with only cats and dogs, but all pets are dirty. If not cared for, they may damage the property in which they are kept. Most companies don't classify a bird as a pet, but a parakeet allowed to fly loose in an apartment can be as dirty as a cat or a dog. Most of us at one time or another have had a beloved cat or dog and then grieved its loss, but we must realize that cats and dogs drop hair, have fleas and mites, carry in dirt from the outside, soil carpets and scratch furniture and woodwork. Nearly every lease, and most rental agreements, will have a clause denying the tenant a pet on the premises.

Some apartment houses stick to this rule; many, however, are more flexible and will allow pets by special written permission in the form of an amendment to the lease or rental agreement and payment of a fee for eventual fumigation and cleaning of the apartment.

PETTY CASH

The resident manager of a very large complex (over 100 units) will more than likely be given a "petty cash fund." This money is to be used for buying small items needed for repair and maintenance – new keys, ashtrays for the recreation room, special office supply, stamps, etc. In the smaller buildings the need for minor items is less, and the company may prefer that the resident manager buy these items as he needs them and be reimbursed on a monthly basis. The resident manager should then know approximately how much money he should spend each month, what items he should spend it on, and what items may be furnished by the company.

RENT COLLECTION

Most companies find it much easier to prorate the rent as each new tenant moves into a building so that all rents are due on the first day of the month. For example if a tenant moves into a building on the fifteenth day of the month, he will pay his deposit and the last fifteen days of the month's rent. Then his rent will be due again on the first day of the following month for that month. Rent is always paid one month in advance. In smaller buildings the rent period may start on the day of the month the tenant moves in. This makes it necessary for the resident manager to be on the alert throughout the month for rent-paying (and delinquent) tenants. If all rent falls due on the first day of the month, then the first five days of the month can be the rent-paying period, and the rest of the month can be devoted to past-due rent, renting vacant apartments, maintenance, service requests, bookkeeping, public relations, etc., etc.

It would seem that if the company arbitrarily prorates the rent at the beginning of a tenancy, the tenant should have the same privilege at his termination of the tenancy. However, many companies do not agree with this, and if improper notice is given by a tenant, will force him to pay an extra month's rent.

Regardless of when the rent is due, it is past due the following day, since there is no legal grace period for the paying of rent. Most companies, however, give the tenant five to ten days. Some companies will impose a late charge of five to ten dollars if the rent is paid at a later date. This is not being unkind of unfair, as it may seem. Past due rent is really a loan from company to tenant. Paying for the roof over our heads is the first debt we should see to each month. Negligence or tardiness in this respect only creates hardships and shortages for others.

If the rent is not paid within five days of the date due, the following day the diligent resident manager will make a call on the delinquent and very nicely ask him when he may expect the rent. This procedure has many advantages. It will enable the resident manager to become acquainted with tenants he has never talked with. It will enable him to enter and inspect an apartment for damage or misuse without the tenant being aware of his inspection. It might show up cause for concern in which the resident manager could be of help and gain a lasting friend. After calling on all past-due tenants for several months, the resident manager will find that more and more of the tenants are paying their rent on time. This eases his job and gets the rents collected earlier in the month. This way the company can know how much money to depend on for the month and thus can budget repairs and other needs of the building more expeditiously.

When a tenant moves in, you as resident manger should inform him never to slip his rent under your door. Tell him that you might not find it, and that if he cannot prove he has paid the rent by his canceled check with your company's endorsement or by a receipt signed by you, you must consider the rent unpaid. The rent should be handed directly to the resident manager or clerk and the tenant issued a receipt at that time. Sometimes a tenant decides to mail the rent. Most people know enough not to send cash through the mail, but if cash is sent and does not arrive, the same rule should apply. Always be available during the rent-paying period.

SHOWING YOUR BUILDING TO OTHERS THAN PROSPECTS

Real Estate Salespeople. Real estate salespeople can be good friends of the resident manager and a fruitful source of prospective tenants. Many times people move into an area and do not want to buy a house or invest in property. They want to have time to live in the area, know the schools, shopping areas, residential areas, get acquainted with some new friends and settled in a new job. These people very often contact the real estate firm for information on rental property. The real estate salesperson will gladly spend some time in helping a prospective renter for he knows that in perhaps a year that person may be looking for a house to buy. Furthermore, real estate agents are normally paid a small commission, set by the state board of realtors, by the company for bringing a renter to its building.

Real estate salespeople are usually very courteous and call in advance to let the resident manager know that they will be bringing a rental prospect; however, there are times when the salesperson is unable to call and will bring his prospect in without prior notice. In a situation like this, the resident manager should show the prospect the apartments for rent as he would any other prospect. He should remember, however, that he is the trained rental agent and keep control of the situation; that is, he should not let the real estate agent take over the selling job for him.

Sometimes a real estate agent will sincerely wish to look at your apartments with the idea of renting some of them for you. Many companies prefer that permission for this kind of showing come directly from the company, so it is wise for the resident manager to know and understand the company's ruling on this. If the real estate agent is sincere and honest, he will not mind your telling him diplomatically that he must first have his permission. He realizes that an apartment house is private property, and that unauthorized persons should not be there.

Fire inspectors. The fire departments of most cities conduct routine inspections of buildings in their areas for the safety of the tenants and the protection of the owners. They will inspect furnaces, wiring, areas in which garbage is thrown, storage areas. These inspections come under a program of fire prevention. The inspectors should be in uniform and should show their credentials. The resident manger should treat these men with courtesy and kindness; they render a valuable service.

Policemen. There are times when policemen or other law-enforcing agents, such as FBI agents, will have occasion to seek entry to an occupied apartment. Such a person should show his credential and a duly drawn search warrant. If he has shown the resident manager a search warrant, and the manager deems it to be valid, he has no alternative but to allow entry, but only to the particular property described in the search warrant. If the person has no search warrant, you should politely tell him he must first obtain permission to enter the apartment from your company's property manager. Honest, upright law-enforcement agents know the law and will not ask you to go against instructions from your company.

Shoppers. The apartment rental industry is highly competitive. Consequently a company must know at all times what its competition is doing-whether the rent is being pushed up or pushed down, what facilities are being offered, how clean the units are, and how large. The company needs to know the over-all picture of the vacancy factor. They need this information in order to gauge the market at a particular time, so that they can be well informed when making recommendations for further investment by the owners, or for lowering or raising rent. Companies don't like to get involved in a price war, but it stands to reason that if two apartment houses are close to each other, offer approximately the same facilities and services, and one of them is selling apartments at appreciably lower rents, that one has a greater advantage of the other. Because concerns that do market surveys often charge high fees and the rental market changes so rapidly that surveys have to be done almost continuously. Most companies choose to do to their own comparison shopping, as it is called.

This comparison shopping is done by the property manager or one of his employees. He usually compares apartment houses somewhat more or less like one or more houses of his own company and located in the same general area. The "shopper," as he is called, presents himself to the resident manager of the competitions' building as a prospective tenant and is shown the building, several apartments, the grounds and the facilities, and is given the rental structure. He will try to find some method of estimating the vacancy factor in the building. With this information he can evaluate the general market and give his company something better than just a guess when he makes his recommendations.

The resident manager himself would find it valuable to shop nearby apartments. He will then be better able to anticipate some of the reasons prospective tenants may give for not renting his apartments and to call attention to things the competition does not offer.

If the resident manager thinks he spots a shopper, he should go along with the shopper's game of playing prospect. Usually, though, the resident manager will never know he has been shopped.

Insurance Agent, Company Personnel and Investors. When renewing the insurance on an apartment house, the insurance company will send a representative to inspect the property. Occasionally insurance personnel not known to the resident manager will want to see the property for various reasons. These people should carry with them a letter of introduction from the company or the property manager, and should identify themselves to you the resident manager before looking around the property. Otherwise, you have every right to accost them, ask them what their business is, and if not satisfied, order them off the property.

HIRING EXTRA HELP

Most companies realize how much work is involved in keeping up any particular property and will see that the resident manager has help where and when it is needed. The resident manager is generally responsible for cleaning the vacated apartments, for which he is paid an hourly wage in addition to the base salary. If, for some reason, he cannot do all that work himself, he should be allowed to hire another person to clean for him. The resident manger would then be the employer, just the same as if he were living in his own house, and would be responsible for seeing that the cleaning was done according to company specifications, and would use the wage paid him to pay his employee. While this could be done rather offhandedly, most companies want to be informed if the resident manager is hiring extra help.

CLEANING AND PAINTING OF OCCUPIED UNITS

It is rather taken for granted that if an apartment is painted, draperies are cleaned, carpeting is shampooed and all appliancies are in working order when the apartment is rented, it is the tenant's responsibility to keep the apartment clean, clean the draperies, shampoo the carpet and replace light bulbs during his occupancy. Very few companies, however, will permit the tenant to do any painting in his apartment, and those that might permit it will want to approve the color of paint. However, the resident manager will find that some companies will clean draperies and carpets for long-term tenants, particularly in a declining market, in order to create good will and retain the tenancy. In a rising market, with a high occupancy rate and few vacancies, companies tend to be more negligent in their public relations.

The decision whether or not to allow the resident manager to paint, shampoo carpets or clean drapery varies so widely among companies that it is almost impossible to state a general policy or rule.

RESIDENT MANAGER'S APARTMENT

It seems to be the notion of most builders that apartment houses with less than 100 (and sometimes more) units do not need a special space for an office. Consequently, a manger usually finds that his apartment becomes the rental office and all prospects and tenants must walk into his living room in order to rent an apartment, sign a rental agreement or pay rent. The resident manger is in essence living in a fishbowl; his apartment is practically public property and he has little or no privacy. (It is my opinion that even the smallest apartment house should have specially built units for the resident manager. There should be a separate space for office use, however small; the manager's apartment should always be a two-bedroom unit, have just a little something the other units may not have and be located for the best access and view of the entire property. It should have an entrance separate from the office entrance.)

The resident manager's apartment, as things now are, become a concern to his company. It must always be as if cleaned for guests - ashtrays emptied, dishes washed, bathroom sparkling. There must never be any drinking of alcoholic beverages in evidence. There must be no slouching on the living-room couch to watch television. Children must be under control at all times. If the resident manager's apartment is dirty and cluttered, most of the prospects will leave, without looking at an apartment for rent, thinking that every apartment must look like the manager's. It may not seem quite fair, but until builders are convinced to the contrary, that is the way it is.

RESIDENT MANAGER'S PERSONAL GROOMING

A resident manager's day usually begins at nine in the morning and theoretically ends at five in the evening. But many people have no time to pay the rent or look for a place to live except after five. Hence the resident manager and his wife should be well groomed and neat appearing until they retire for the night. The manager's wife should have her hair out of rollers and combed, and her make-up on by nine in the morning. If she is not attractive in slacks, she should be in a dress. All manager's wives should avoid wearing shorts or dresses that are extremely short; the resident managers of apartment houses are constantly coming in contact with strangers, and the habit of showing off much of the body is simply unwise. When the wife is cleaning vacated apartments, she can be expected to be in slacks; however, women do wait on tables, clean motel rooms and do all sorts of labor in dresses (uniforms) without any problem. If the woman is not attractive in slacks, she can wear a housedress when she is doing cleaning. Nothing looks worse than worn-out slacks, fuzzy house slippers, and hair in rollers, even if the woman is slim and young. The husband should always be clean-shaven and have his hair combed. In the larger complex where there is a rental office, the wife (or other woman tending the office) should always be dressed as she would be in a downtown office. The husband can be neatly dressed in a sport coat, or in shirt sleeves in summer weather.

Let the atmosphere of the building show in your manner of dress. If you have a resort type of place, wear sporty clothes. Whatever you may be wearing, be sure you look right in it, and keep yourself neat and well groomed at all times you are likely to come in contact with tenants or prospective tenants.

CHAPTER V

FORMS, FORMS, AND MORE FORMS

The sample forms shown at the end of this chapter are neither identical with nor greatly different from the forms actually used in the management of apartment houses. They are, rather, representative composites.

The text of legal forms has been left out, as these will vary from state to state and company to company. No one company will use all the forms included.

Many companies do not require that their resident manager keep copies of all forms he sends to them. It is nevertheless a good practice for him to have a personal file of every such slip of paper or notation. This will be his own personal file and should go with him when he leaves that particular apartment house, as it is a record of his work there and what he has done. Also, things do get lost in the mail and in company offices at times; if the manager has kept an extra copy for himself, he will always be able to supply the needed duplicate.

The card file that he has kept for the company and his apartment house should stay at the apartment house, so that the next resident manager will have accurate records of maintenance. Unless the resident manager has made extra copies of rental agreements and leases for his own file, these also should remain at the apartment house and be passed on.

APPLICATION FOR RENTAL

The application for rental is really a credit form and a means by which the resident manager can "qualify" his prospective tenant. There are national statistics that show how much a person can afford to pay in rent out of his income. The rule of thumb is that a person can afford to pay one-fourth of his monthly income, after any long-term installments (six months or longer) have been deducted. For example: if the head of the household earns $1,000 a month before taxes and has no other payments each month, he should be able to pay $250 a month for rent. If he has an installment loan of $150 a month on an automobile that has six months or more to go, the $150 must be deducted from the $1,000 and the remainder of $850 must be divided by 4 which would enable him to pay $212 a month for rent. If two single persons are to share an apartment, their combined incomes are taken into account. Companies usually feel they would rather not rent unless the prospective tenant can truly afford the rent they ask, since they would risk the rents being paid late or not at all.

Many smaller apartment houses do not use the application for rental. The resident manager is responsible, from knowledge he has acquired first hand, for qualifying the prospective tenant. In many large complexes the application form is used as a matter of course and must be filled out by every tenant upon renting. Sometimes a short credit reference is included with the rental agreement or lease.

APARTMENT LEASE

A lease is a contract to possess and use something for a given length of time at a definite cost, and its duration can be from a few months to ninety-nine years.

The apartment lease is widely used and is usually of one year's duration, the exceptions being in the very high-priced units. To the tenant, the lease means that he must pay a certain price each month for his apartment for the duration of the lease. If the rent structure moves higher in the area, the tenant knows that he will not have to pay a higher rent for the duration of his lease. On the other hand, if the rent structure moves down, the tenant is still obligated to pay the rent shown in his lease for the duration. Hence the lease can be a disadvantage or an advantage to both tenant and landlord. When the lease has expired, the tenant must either vacate his apartment or renew his lease for another definite period.

The lease should be dated the same day it is signed. The Lessor is the company, and the Lessee is the tenant. Married tenants' signature should include both given names – "John J. and Mary H. Doe"; the signature for two single parties sharing an apartment should give both full names. The lease should state the apartment number; the full name of the apartment house and its address, including city, county and state; the number of adults and of children and all the children's full names. The term of the lease is the number of months, with the date the lease begins and the date it expires. The amount of rent should be written out – "Two Hundred and Fifty and no/100 Dollars" – then written again in figures - $250.00." Rent is always payable in advance on a certain day of the month. If the rent is prorated so that it will fall on the first day of the month, the next line, "The payment of" (the written-out amount of money first being paid) might state the first one-half month's rent plus the last month's rent, which is often collected with the lease. If a deposit is collected with the first and last months' rent, it should be a separate item and so designated. It will then be signed by the Lessor and the Lessee. The resident manager may be given the power to sign for his company; he will then write the company's name and under it will sign his own name, as "His Agent."

RENTAL AGREEMENT

The rental agreement is used even more widely than the lease in apartment-house management. It is usually simple and easier to understand. There may be some forfeiture if the apartment is vacated within a certain length of time. There will be the date, full names of tenants, amount of the deposit, apartment number and name of apartment house and its address.

This form gives space for the rent amount in figures only; many forms require the written-out amount also. Again, there are the number of adults and children and all the children's names. There will be a lot of fine print in some forms, or just a few, easily read lines in others. The rent commences on the date both the resident manager and tenant have agreed upon; there are given one reference by the tenant, his occupation and his last address. The tenants both sign, the company's name is put on the Lessor's line, and the resident manager signs after the word "by" as "His Agent."

AUTHORIZATION FOR PET

Nearly all leases and rental agreements will have a clause in them to the effect that no animals are to be kept in the apartments. Companies in general would like not to allow any animals in their buildings, but they realize they cannot always have prospects without pets and cannot require that prospective tenants dispose of beloved pets in order to rent their apartments, especially if there is a high vacancy factor. Since the original agreement says, "no pets," the Authorization for Pet form must be an amendment to that agreement, and the tenant makes an additional deposit, non-refundable, for the fumigation and cleaning of that apartment when he vacates. The first line will describe the original agreement, that is, "lease," or "rental agreement." Then there will be the apartment number and apartment house name and address. There will be a line for the complete description, and the name of the pet, an agreement to the deposit, date, and signature of company, resident manager and tenant. There will be a few clauses stating that the tenant agrees to pay for any damages caused by the pet and that the agreement may be canceled by the resident manager if he deems it necessary. Most companies place a size and weight limit on pets, in addition to a limit on the number of pets that may be kept by a tenant.

FURNITURE INVENTORY

The furniture inventory of a furnished apartment should be attached to the lease or rental agreement. The apartment should be inspected by the tenant and the resident manager, the inventory made together, and notations made concerning any damage or lack of cleanliness in the furnishings. There will be the apartment house name and the date the inventory was made, and the paper will be signed by both tenant and manager. If a resident manager has a building catering to weekly rentals, the inventory might include linen and kitchen equipment.

CARD FOR CARD FILE

If the resident manager who preceded you does not have a card file on the apartments in the building, then you should start one. On the front of the card there should be the apartment number, name of tenant, his occupancy date and his vacating date. This way you have a running record of the occupancy of each apartment. On the reverse side of the card you should note everything that is done in the apartment and the date on which the work was completed. Don't skimp; put down anything you feel is important to remember about that particular apartment. When you have used all the space on the first card, attach another to it with a stapler. Do not destroy any card. After a few years there will be a running history of each apartment in your building. This card file should pass from manager to manager, so turn it over to the new manager when you leave.

WEEKLY TRAFFIC REPORT

The resident manager is required to keep a record of all the prospective tenants he receives, find out how they happened to stop at his building, and if he doesn't rent to them, try to find out why. The report is sent to the company at the end of each week. From the traffic reports the company will build statistics that enable them to evaluate certain advertising and to make better recommendations to its investors.

REPORT OF COLLECTIONS

This is a record of the rents, deposits and pet fees (or any other money you may collect). If your rent is picked up by the property manager or his employee, this form might accompany each day's collections, with the totals balanced at the bottom. If you are required to make deposits each time you have collected money, the totals should equal the deposit, and the collection report sent to the company. If the rents are picked up, the resident manager should receive a receipt from the person doing the collecting, for the total amount of money each time it is collected. Some companies will use a form such as this only once a month, and it will show the total collection for the month.

DELINQUENCY REPORT

This report shows which tenants are past due in paying rent and gives the company information to use in their attempts to collect. It also shows how much is past due and keeps the company abreast of which tenants tend to be late. It shows what action you have taken in attempting to collect past-due rents and has a method of balancing so that your figures are correct.

COLLECTION REPORT ON EVICTIONS AND SKIPS

Persons evicted from apartments are often tenants who have not paid their rent for a couple of months; consequently, when they do vacate, they still owe back rent. There are also those who try to get around paying rent by moving out in the middle of the night or in some other sneaky way. These people are called "skips." Generally this past-due rent is collected by the company itself, but where the resident manager is responsible for the collection, he will use this form.

VACANCY REPORT

This is a report very valuable to the company. It may be required of the resident manager once a week or once a month. It enables the company to see at a glance the vacancy factor of your building. If trouble is spotted, the company can promptly look for the reason, perhaps locate the problem, solve it and not lose any more tenants.

MAINTENANCE REQUEST

This form can be used by either the resident manager or the property manager. It helps route the work to be done and the priority given to each job. A copy should be kept by the resident manager and notations made when each job is completed. It should then be transferred to the card file on his building. In this way a running file is kept on all the maintenance done in each apartment and the date it is completed.

NOTICE OF INTENTION TO VACATE

This notice is filled out and presented to the resident manager by the tenant to the effect that he intends to vacate his apartment on such and such a date. Nearly every state has certain laws set forth for the tenant to give a certain length of notice. The laws of your state will usually be included in the text of the form. After the notice is filled out by the tenant and presented, the resident manager then signs it and sends a copy to his company. The form will also state that the apartment to be vacated can be shown for rent by the resident manager before it is vacated.

DEPOSIT REFUND

The deposit refund form is filled out by the resident manager as soon as possible after the apartment is vacated. This form determines how much of the former tenant's deposit is to be refunded to him. It is important that this form go to the company just as soon as the resident manager can get the apartment cleaned. Tenants who have to wait for their deposits to be refunded can become very irate.

NOTICE TO VACATE REPORT

This form will list all Notices to Vacate the resident manager has received in a given period. Your company may require this information sent in once a week or once a month. It gives your company information from which he might make projections on the amount of income that may be expected in the months ahead. It also gives the reasons for tenants' desires to vacate apartments and could show a trend, or problems in management that the company can see to quickly and perhaps remedy.

CASH EXPENDTIURES AND ITEMS CHARGED TO COMPANY

In some cases the resident manager is given a petty cash fund, as has been mentioned. In other cases the manager is instructed to spend his own money and send a statement to the company for reimbursement. There are also times when the resident manager is given the power to charge certain items at certain business houses. For all cash purchases there must be a receipt attached to the form, and every charge must have a copy of the invoice so that the bookkeepers can cross-check the purchases, ascertain that they are valid, and keep them on file. The Internal Revenue Service requires that there be a receipt for any item that is deducted as an operating expense. This form can be used whether or not the resident manager is given an advance of petty cash.

REQUEST FOR PETTY CASH REIMBURSEMENT

This form is for use when the resident manager has had petty cash advanced to him by his company. It is in the form of a small statement of finance. It shows how much money has been advanced, the amounts spent and what they have been spent for. It then shows how much is left of the petty cash advanced (or it may show that the resident manager has spent some of his own money in addition) and the amount of petty cash required for the following period. When petty cash is advanced, it is usually done by the month and the resident manager's cash statement, whichever form is used, is sent in on a monthly basis. Again, all receipts should be attached to the form.

REQUEST FOR ISSUANCE OF CHECK

If the company has given the resident manager authority to hire needed help, or if the company itself keeps extra help for maintaining the grounds or for cleaning rooms, it will be the responsibility of the resident manager to supervise the persons doing the work, report their hours to the company and request that checks be issued to those persons. Checks may be mailed to the resident manager for distribution to his employees or may be mailed directly to the employees. There will be full explanations of the work done and the hours worked. It is also possible that the resident manager has been given permission to buy an item too large to take from petty cash and at a place of business where his company does not have an account. This form would then be used in order for the resident manager to receive the check and pay for the items at the time of purchase.

NOTICE TO PAY RENT OR VACATE; NOTICE TO TERMINATE TENANCY

These forms are most generally used by the company and served on the tenant by a representative of the company other than the resident manager. They are included here only to familiarize you with such forms.

41

DUPLICATE CHECK REGISTER

This form will be used only when the resident manager is doing the full job of managing an apartment house - that is, collecting rents, depositing the monies and paying the bills. He will keep an accurate account of all checks issued, in duplicate, and the original will go to the accountant who does the accounting each month, along with duplicate deposit slips showing the income of the apartment house being managed.

CHECKING ACCOUNT DEPOSIT SLIP

The long-form deposit slip issued by banks gives room for listing a number of items (checks); the cash is broken down into bills of each denomination and coin. There is a double number in the upper right-hand corner of each check. The top number is hyphenated and the lower is single. It is the hyphenated number that is used on the deposit slip when listing checks. When all the cash, coin, and checks have been listed, the total amount of the deposit is written at the bottom of the slip. These deposit forms are always made in duplicate; the original goes to the bank and the duplicate to the accountant.

APARTMENT HOUSE RULES AND REGULATIONS

Apartment house rules and regulations will vary widely from apartment house to apartment house, company to company, and city to city. The list given here could all be used or partly used or added to, but it will give the prospective resident manager some idea of the rules and regulations he may be enforcing.

RENT RECEIPT

Rent receipts are usually standard forms. There will be date, name of person paying the rent, apartment number and amount paid. The amount will be written out and again in figures. The form will show the period for which the rent is being paid and the medium of exchange (cash, check, money order, etc.) used in paying it. The resident manager signs on the bottom line. Receipts are usually made in triplicate; the original is given to the tenant, the duplicate sent to the company and the triplicate kept by the resident manager. When the first month's rent is collected, along with the security deposit, it is wise to make separate receipts so it can be readily seen that one is for rent and the other for deposit.

SUPPLY REQUISITION

This is really an order blank for supplies needed by the resident manager. However, by his showing the amounts he has on hand, his property manager can add these to his inventory in stock and keep abreast at all times of the supplies he has on hand. The form will also show how much of certain items are being used and thus whether or not they are being wasted.

These forms should be made in duplicate and the duplicate kept by the resident manager. When the supplies are delivered, he should check them against his order, make note they were received, and initial his receipt for the person delivering them.

SAMPLE FORMS (SEE FOLLOWING PAGES)

APPLICATION FOR RENTAL

Name _____ Age ___ Wife's
Name _____

Soc Sec
No. _____ Single ___Married ___Divorced ___ Dependents:
No. __ Ages __

Wife's
Former Name _____ Soc Sec
No. _____

Address _____ How Long Own_____Rent___

Former
Address _____ How Long Own_____Rent___
Address

Employer _____ Employed_____

Position _____ Since _____

Income _____ Per _____

Bank References _____ Branch _____

CREDIT REFERENCES

Dept. Store _____ Fuel _____

Dept. Store _____ Furniture _____

Apparel _____ Dentist _____

Jewelry _____ Physician _____

Other _____ Other _____

PERSONAL REFERENCES

1. _____ Address _____

2. _____ Address _____

3. _____ Address _____

Address of Property to be Rented
_____ Date

Applicant's
Signature _____

APARTMENT LEASE

THIS INDENTURE OF LEASE, made in triplicate this _____day of _____, 19 _____, by and between _____ _____, hereinafter called the Lessor, and _____ _____, hereinafter called the Lessee:

WITNESSETH:

1. Lessor, in consideration of the rents, covenants and agreement hereinafter set form to be paid and performed by Lessee, does hereby lease and demise unto said Lessee, and said Lessee does hereby accept, lease and take from said Lessor, Apartment No. _____, hereinafter referred to as the "demised premises," in the apartment house known as _____, being numbered ____in the City of _____, County,____ _____, to be occupied as and for a dwelling, and for no other purpose, solely by ____ adults and ____children, consisting of _____ for a term of ____months from _____ to _____, inclusive.

2. Lessee agrees to pay as rental for said apartment the sum of _____ Dollars ($_____) per month, in lawful money of the United States of America, payable in advance on or before the _____ day of each and every month during the full term of this lease. The payment of _____now made, shall, in the event of the full and faithful performance by the Lessee of all the covenants, agreements and terms in this lease by the Lessee to be kept and performed, be credited in payment of the first and _____ month's rent of said term; but otherwise said payment this day made shall belong to the Lessor as a part of the consideration to Lessor for the exclusion of this Lease.

   IN WITNESS WHEREOF, the parties hereto have executed this lease, the day and year first above written.

_____	_____
Lessor	Lessee
_____	_____
His Agent	Lessee

RENTAL AGREEMENT

_____, 19_____

RECEIVED OF _____hereinafter
called the Tenant, the sum of $_____, as a deposit
on the rent of apartment number _____, _____
_____ Apartments, _____; said rental to
be $_____ per week/month, and the Tenant agrees to
pay said rental in advance.

In consideration of the strict performance of all the terms and
conditions of this Rental Agreement by the Tenant, said premises
are rented to the Tenant for the occupancy solely by _____
adults and _____ children, consisting of _____

Rent to commence _____, 19 _____

TENANT'S REFERENCE:

_____   _____
                                  Tenant

Tenant's Occupation _____ _____
                                  Tenant

Last Residence Address _____

_____   _____
                                  Lessor

          By _____
                                  His Agent

46

AUTHORIZATION FOR PET

It is understood that this Authorization for Pet is an amendment of your _____. In consideration of the execution of this Amendment, and subject to the conditions herein, the Lessor agrees to permit the Lessee to keep a pet in Apartment No. _____, of the _____ Apartments, at _____ _____ State.   Lessee agrees that said permission is restricted to the following pet and that no other pet will be brought in or kept without the written approval of the Lessor:

_____

Lessee agrees to make a $ _____, non-refundable deposit, which is attached hereto.
IN WITNESS WHEREOF the parties have executed this Amendment this _____day of _____, 19 _____

_____
Lessor

_____
His Agent

_____
Lessee

CARD FOR CARD FILE

Tenant Name	Occupancy Date	Vacating Date

FURNITURE INVENTORY

Name of Building _____Date
, 19

Apartment Number _____

LIVING ROOM   BEDROOM

_____Sofa   _____ Box Spring
_____Cocktail Table   _____ Headboard
_____Table Lamp   _____ Dresser
_____Occasional Chair   _____ Mirror
                               _____ Night Stand
                               _____ Lamps

DINING ROOM
_____Table
_____Chairs

Tenant hereby accepts above listed articles in good condition and agrees to pay for all damaged or missing articles.

(Signed) _____
Tenant

(Signed)_____
Tenant

(Signed)_____
Resident Manager

WEEKLY TRAFFIC REPORT

Name of Apartment _____

Resident Manager _____

Date

Apartment Showings
Sunday _____
Monday _____
Tuesday _____
Wednesday _____
Thursday _____
Friday _____
Saturday _____

Total _____

Rented
1 Bedroom _____
2 Bedroom _____
3 Bedroom _____
Studio _____

Source of Prospects
Newspaper

_____
_____
_____
Yellow Pages _____
Drop Ins _____
Outdoor Signs _____
Referral _____
Total _____
Other _____

Reasons for Not Renting
Units too Small _____
Poor Location _____
Rent Too High _____
Deposit Too High _____
Lack of Facilities _____
What _____
_____
Undesirable Prospect _____
Other _____

Remarks: _____
_____
_____
_____

REPORT OF COLLECTIONS

Apartment Name _____Month _____

Resident Manager_____Year _____

Day	Apt. #	Tenant's Name	Deposit (1)	Rent (2)	Pet Fee (3)	Total (4)
TOTALS						

To Balance: (1) + (2) + (3) must equal (4).

DELINQUENCY REPORT

Apartment Name _____Date

Resident Manager _____

Unit #	Tenant Name	Prev Month (1)	Curr Month (2)	Late Chgs (3)	Total (4)	Action taken & Date will Pay
Total Amount Due						

To Balance: (1) + (2) + (3) must equal (4)

COLLECTION REPORT

EVICTIONS AND SKIP ACCOUNTS

Apartment Name _____Date

Resident Manager _____

Unit #	Name	Reason	Move Out Date	Amount Due	Date of Collection	Remarks

Total Amount Due		

VACANCY REPORT

Apartment Name _____Date

Resident Manager _____

Unit #	Bedrooms			Date Vacated	Rent	Deposit	Occupancy Date	Remarks
	1	2	3					

TOTAL	Total Vacant Units		

Less Vacant Units with Deposits _____
Total Units not committed _____

MAINTENANCE REQUEST

Maintenance Requested by _____   Date _____ , 19 ___
Apartment Name _____   Address _____
Resident Manager _____   Phone _____

Unit No.	No. Bdrms	Occpd Vent	Tenant Name	Crpt Clng	Drpy Clng	Paint	Repairs	Instr	Date Cmpltd

Maintenance Authorized by _____   Date _____ , 19 ___

Remarks _____
_____

NOTICE OF INTENTION TO VACATE

TO: _____, LESSOR, _____APARTMENTS.
YOU ARE HEREBY NOTIFIED that the undersigned tenants,
apartment number _____, will vacate said premises on or
before _____, 19 _____, and you may show said
premises for sale or rental at all reasonable times from this date
forward.

Dated this _____day of _____, 19 _____

_____
Lessee

_____
Lessee

_____
Lessee

Received _____, 19 _____

_____
Lessor

_____
His Agent

DEPOSIT REFUND

Apartment Name _____   Date Moved In
Address _____   Date Moved Out
Apartment No. _____   Started Cleaning ____
Tenant Name _____   Finished Cleaning ____
Forwarding Address _____
Was proper notice to vacate given? _____
Was all rent paid up to date? _____
Were all keys turned in? _____
Was there any physical damage to the apartment? _____
Describe _____

Do carpets need cleaning? _____   TIME SPENT CLEANING
Do draperies need cleaning? _____   Range _____hrs.
Were any light globes missing? _____   Refrigerator ____hrs.
Does furniture need cleaning? _____   Dishwasher _____hrs.
                                          Walls _____hrs.
                                          Floors _____ hrs.
                                          Bathroom _____hrs.
                                          General _____ hrs.
                                          TOTAL _____hrs.

To be Paid to Resident Manager $ _____

_____
Resident Manager

NOTICE TO VACATE REPORT

Apartment Name _____Date
Resident Manager _____

Unit #	No. bdrms-1	2	3	Date of Notice	Vacate Date	Reason for Vacating

Total				Total no. vacating

CASH EXPENDITURES

Apartment Name _____Date
Resident Manager _____For month of _____

Date	To Whom Paid	Item Purchased	Amount Paid

ITEMS CHARGED TO COMPANY

Date	Item Charged	Co. Charged to	Invoice #	Amount

Attach cash receipts and copies of invoices

REQUEST FOR PETTY CASH REIMBURSEMENT

Date   19

Apartment Name _____

Resident Manager _____

AMOUNT OF PETTY CASH FORWARDED $ _____

Disbursements:

_____$
_____$
_____$

Total Disbursements $_____   ($)
    Remainder of Petty Cash Fund $
    Reimbursement Requested $

Signed _____
        Resident Manager
All receipts must be attached to this report

REQUEST FOR ISSUANCE OF CHECK

Date _____ , 19 _____

Make check payable to _____

In the amount of _____

Mail to _____

Address _____

_____

Explanation _____

_____

_____

_____

Requested by _____

Resident Manager

Apartment _____

NOTICE TO PAY RENT OR VACATE

To _____ You
and each of you are hereby notified and informed that the rent for
the _____ ending on the _____ day of _____
_____, 19 _____, for the certain premises situated in the County
of _____, State of _____, and
more particularly described as follows, to wit: _____
_____is now due and payable in the sum of __
_____DOLLARS. And you are hereby notified and required
to pay the same to the undersigned or his agent named below,
within three days from date of the service of this notice upon you,
or in the alternative to vacate and surrender said premises.

Dated this _____day of _____, 19 _____

_____

Owner

By_____

His Agent

_____

Address

NOTICE TO TERMINATE TENANCY

To _____

You are hereby notified that the tenancy of the premises occupied by you as tenant of the undersigned owner, described as follows, to wit: _____, in the County of ___ _____, State of -_____, is hereby terminated on the _____ day of _____, 19 _____, and that on said day you will be required by these presents to surrender the possession of said premises to said owner or his agent named below. In default thereof proceedings will be commenced to dispossess you and to gain possession of said premises.

Dated at _____, County, _____, this _____
Day of _____, 19 _____

_____
Owner

By _____
Agent

DUPLICATE CHECK REGISTER

Apartment Name _____ Page ____ of _____ Pages

Resident Manager _____
For the Month of _____, 19 _____

Date	Check #	Check Issued to	Check Amount	Deposit Amount	Balance	Remarks

CHECKING ACCOUNT DEPOSIT
CITY NATIONAL BANK

City, State

Date   Acct. No. _____

Name _____

Address _____

	Number	Dollars	Cents
1.00 bills			
5.00 bills			
10.00 bills			
20.00 bills			
Coin			
List Checks Separately			
Total Deposit			

APARTMENT HOUSE RULES
AND REGULATIONS
RENT MUST BE PAID IN ADVANCE

1. A deposit will be required on each key furnished to Tenant – money refunded when key is turned in.

2. Management not responsible for fire, theft, or damage to personal effects, in apartment, laundry, storage lockers,

garage or any portion of the building. Keep your apartment door locked at all times.

3. Only the number of persons, and specific persons, designated in the Rental Agreement shall occupy the apartment without written consent of the Lessor. Apartments may not be sublet without written consent of the Lessor.

4. All bills must be paid before baggage and furniture are removed. Checks not acceptable for final bill

5. The management reserves the right to enter any apartment at all reasonable times and reserves the right to show an apartment after notice has been given.

6. No domestic animals allowed in the building without written permission of management.

7. Children not permitted to play in the halls, the stairways, the entrances, or in or around the elevator.

8. No loud talking or unnecessary noise permitted in apartment or halls. Noise of every description must cease at 10:30 p.m. No piano, radio, or other musical instrument to be played before 8:30 a.m. or later than 10:30 p.m. No teaching of music, either vocal or instrumental, is permitted.

9. Tenants will be required to pay for all breakages, and for all damage done to the furniture, rugs, dishes, window shades or building.

10. Tenants must not throw anything or shake dust mops out of window.

11. Do not use water on hardwood floors; they should be waxed and polished.

12. Water shall not be left running in the kitchen, bathroom, laundry or elsewhere. Report any defects in the plumbing to the manager. Tenants will be required to pay for damage to plumbing due to their neglect.

13. Do not open windows unnecessarily. Comply strictly with all heating regulations issued from time to time by the management.

14. No tacks or nails may be put in the walls or woodwork.

15. Tenants vacating will be charged for soiled linen, curtains, blankets and comforters. Linen charges at regular price of laundry doing housework.

16. A charge will be made for moving from one apartment to another.

17. When vacating apartment a charge will be made for cleaning of same, unless left in condition satisfactory to the manager.

18. All complaints or requests should be left with the manager.

19. No changes in any fixture or wiring or alteration to apartment will be permitted without written permission of the manager.

20. All litter cans must be kept clean and all garbage and other refuse must be wrapped.

21. Persons renting by the week required to give seven days' notice of intention to vacate.

22. The use of the laundry room may be denied any tenant who causes unpleasantness therein or who disregards the rules pertaining thereto.

23. Tenants are required by state law to give _____ days' notice in writing prior to the expiration of a monthly period, before vacating apartment. Apartment must be vacated by 12 o'clock noon.

RENT RECEIPT

_____ 19_____

Received from _____

_____Dollars
                                          100

From _____ to _____

$ _____ Paid by: Cash _____ Check _____

_____

SUPPLY REQUISITION

Apartment Name _____Date
Address _____
Phone _____

Check if NeededItemAmount on HandAmount Requested

	Light bulbs		
	40 watt		
	60 watt		
	100 watt		
	All purpose cleanser		
	Scouring powder		
	Oven cleaner		
	Aluminum Cleaner		
	Disinfectant		
	Brooms		
	Mops		
	Floor Wax		

ITEMS NOT NORMALLY CARRIED IN STOCK

Describe in full, giving model number and make:

_____

Resident Manager

CHAPTER VI

MANAGER-TENANT RELATIONSHIP

PUBLIC RELATIONS

"Public relations" can be defined as the efforts of a business to interpret itself to its public in a favorable light – that is, to influence people to believe that the business is serving their interests and benefiting them.

After the apartments are rented, the rents collected and the maintenance cared for, the resident manager becomes a public relations man for himself, his apartment house and his company. He attends to service requests, to tenant complaints about other tenants and other tenants' pets or stereos and televisions. He explains his company's policy about maintenance, animals, children, and children's toys. He helps the vacating tenant by explaining the vacating notice and deposit return. He is forever helpful in any way he can find to give service. He is a good listener to other people's problems. He follows the golden rule: "Do unto others as you would have others do unto you." It is his job to renew the leases and make the present tenants want to stay in his building. Most tenants who stay in a building over a long period of time do so because they like the management. To the tenant the resident manager is the management, since the tenants rarely see any other representative of the company. When a tenant brings a friend to rent an apartment or tells the local barber or grocer that your building is the nicest place in your community to live, then you as the resident manager can know you are doing a good job of public relations.

It seems that a sense of public relations comes naturally to some people. If the truth is known, these people have learned a lot of it, perhaps through trial and error, throughout their lives. Most of them have a genuine concern for their fellow men. They really care about people they come in contact with. Their hearts sincerely ache at the tragedy and sorrow they see about them. They tend to find some good in every person, and meet each new person with kindness.. When a person tries to acquire this attitude, however, but doesn't really feel it inside himself, he is usually a failure at public relations.

This kind of relationship cannot be acquired overnight, but it can be practiced with each personal contact. See how many things you can learn about the next person you meet and think of any small thing you may do to make him feel more comfortable. If you learn of some way you can help, offer your service. Time, concern and caring are what I am talking about, not money. After practicing with friends and acquaintances for a few weeks or months, you will realize that it is you who gain. The old adage, "Be good for goodness' sake" still holds true, and the cup of life will hold much golden nectar for you who follow it throughout your lives.

SERVICE REQUESTS

Learning to feel and care takes practice with oneself, yet there are some mechanics of how to deal with certain problems arising in apartment house managing that can help along the way. Tenants should be informed upon renting that anything that may go wrong in their apartments should be reported promptly to the resident manager. They should be told not to put up with leaky faucets or broken plug-ins, since if they don't report such problems, the resident manager cannot know the problems exist. When there is a service request, the resident manager should see that the repair is made quickly, if possible at that very moment. If the repair is out of the jurisdiction of the resident manager, it should be reported to the company with an urgent request it be cared for soon. There are times when the company must rely on a firm, or contract for labor, and this may take longer than the tenant feels necessary for a repair to be made. The resident manager should then explain fully the reason for the delay and assure the tenant that the repair will be made as soon as possible. The manager should always be forthright and honest with his tenants, and he must be decisive in his actions.

Nothing is more destructive to good will than forcing a tenant to make the same request time and time again before a repair is made. If a request is made that is unusual as far as normal service is concerned, make a point of knowing whether or not it can be granted. If it cannot be granted, the tenant should be told so, firmly and courteously. In this way you will have created a friend, for people genuinely respect honesty.

TENANT COMPLAINTS ABOUT OTHER TENANTS OR PETS

Often a resident manager will find he is the mediator between conflicting tenants. Tenant Jones appears at the manager's door and complains that tenant Smith is playing his stereo or television too loud. Jones seems very angry at that moment and the resident manager tends to think that Jones wants him to go right to Smith, give him a bawling out and order him to turn the stereo down. What tenant Jones really wants, as he explains after he has cooled off, is for you to solve the problem without mentioning his name. One way the resident manager can handle this is to walk past tenant Smith's apartment (to verify the complaint), then either knock on the door or go back to your apartment and phone (personal visits are always preferred) and tell Smith you just happened to be walking past his door, it seemed his stereo was rather loud and would he mind lowering it just a bit? Then suggest how he might feel if the situation were reversed. This approach will nearly always work and the resident manager will not have created ill will between tenants by letting it be known that someone has complained.

It may be that a tenant has left a dog in his apartment while gone on a shopping trip and the animal sets up a howl. Neighbor Tillie calls to complain. The resident manager could go past the apartment to check, and perhaps then take the animal to his own apartment, leaving a note to that effect on the tenant's door. When the owner comes home, the resident manager could explain that the dog was howling (as if its heart would break) from being left alone and was so lonesome he just couldn't bear to leave it there. Then he might casually call attention to a clause in the lease or rental agreement stating that animals should not be left alone in apartments. Again, the resident manager has averted ill will between tenants – and what pet lover can resist someone's feeling sorry for his beloved pet? Furthermore, a tenant will take a reprimand for enforcing the rules set by the company, not another tenant. The tenant also knows that he would be treated in like manner if the situation were reversed and appreciates the manager's concern for tenants.

EXPLAINING RULES AND REGULATIONS

A good resident manager will not only explain the rules and regulations which have been set for his building, he will also explain why and how they came about. Many people think rules and regulations are for every person other than themselves, since their children are the best, their pets are never naughty, and their families never create any kind of disturbance. So explain, over and over again, all through the tenancy, why the rules have been made. This establishes a good basic understanding between resident manager and tenants.

VACATING TENANTS AND DEPOSIT RETURN

Tenants should be informed upon renting what is expected of them in the way of cleaning the apartment at the time they vacate. Apartment newly painted, carpet shampooed, draperies cleaned, all appliances in working order – these should be a matter of record in the card file the resident manager keeps on his building. This information should be noted on the rental agreement and the tenant should be told just what he must do in order to have all his deposit refunded. There is wide variation among companies; some want the tenant to do everything but paint, even have a professional carpet cleaner in. Since this could cost more than the amount on deposit, the tenant might just decide to walk away and let the company foot the bill. Other companies would rather have closer control of the carpet cleaning, and so do not charge for it unless there is undue dirt or damage. All cleaning that has to be done when a tenant vacates is charged against the deposit; the balance is returned to the tenant, with an accounting.

It is the responsibility of the resident manager to clean a vacated apartment, keep track of the hours spent and report this to the company. So the manager is the person solely responsible for how much of the deposit is returned to the tenant. Some companies don't like tenants to know that it is the resident manager who has the last word on the refund, thinking that this keeps him protected from irate tenants. Other companies put out memos to vacating tenants stating that the resident manager is solely responsible. If tenants are made fully aware of their responsibilities upon renting, there will be no irate tenants. It is the responsibility of the resident manager to know and understand his own company's policy and work within the rules.

BEING A FRIEND

Be a friend to all your tenants, an intimate to none. Offer help-needle and thread, a cup of sugar. Acknowledge birthdays, anniversaries, births, and deaths with a word, a card, or a deed. Help an unemployed tenant find a lead to a new job (it may be just an ad in the paper that he overlooked), and you may save a tenant. One manager has a coffee-and-cookies party for herself on moving into a new building and invites all the tenants, then informs them there is always a pot of coffee at her apartment during certain hours and they are welcome to come and chat. Some managers always have a pot of coffee or tea, or lemonade and cookies, for prospective tenants while discussing rentals. Some larger complexes have periodic parties around the pool for all tenants. Smaller ones have picnics in the yard. Listen to problems and always be ready to lend a helping hand. Never play favorites or let yourself be seen visiting a certain apartment too often, or other tenants will become envious. Acknowledge a long-term tenant's length of tenancy and state you have enjoyed their tenancy and hope it continues for another long period. Be a friend; you'll never regret it.

CHAPTER VII

SELLING AND SHOWING APARTMENTS

There are many different kinds of selling.

Selling real estate, selling brushes or cosmetics door to door, selling by convincing one of your customers she should have a party to let you show your wares, selling insurance, selling automobiles, selling books, etc. - all of these might be termed direct or outside sales jobs, in that usually the sales agent must seek out and convince the prospect he wants that which he has for sale.

Retailing, wholesaling, distributing, professional services of all kinds that may be advertised or promoted are termed inside sales. Here the prospective buyer comes to the seller, having already decided that he needs or wants certain goods or services that seller is offering.

SELLING ONESELF

The prerequisite to any kind of selling is the selling of oneself. The real estate agent will not sell houses if he complains about the high interest rates, the poor condition of the property or the unfairness of his firm. The door-to-door sales agent will not sell brushes or cosmetics if he grumbles about the weather or having to walk so much. The retail sales clerk will not sell shoes, purses or jewelry by being glum and uninterested in either her merchandise or her customer. So it is with resident managers who are selling apartments.

Almost anyone can be taught to show an apartment. Selling an apartment is an entirely different matter. The selling of an apartment can be called an inside sale in that the prospective tenant has already decided he needs or wants what you have for sale – an apartment. He has come to your building because he wants to be in that general location. He has seen from your signs or advertising that you have the size of apartment he needs, at a price he feels he is able to pay. All this being so, the resident manager must then convince his prospect that he wants a particular apartment in his particular building.

His first job is to sell himself. The first step in selling oneself is to smile. Always be cheerful and always smile. If it is raining say you like the rain – it makes the flowers grow and the lawns green; the farmers really need it and besides, it makes one appreciate the sunshine. And smile. If the sun is shining, be very glad because one always likes nice weather for swimming and picnicking. And smile. The manager who always had a cup of coffee or tea and cookies was selling herself, and smiling. Ask to be called by your first name, and ask if you might address your prospective tenant by his. Don't be afraid to ask questions: "Where have you been living?" "How many children have you?" "Have you a pet?" "Did you last live in a house or apartment?" "Do you like to swim?" "Do you play tennis?" "Go to movies?" Really listen, and have a return remark for each question: "Oh, I know that area. It's a real nice place and the people there are so friendly." "You have three children? I have two, but they're both grown now, and I'm a grandfather." "I lived in a house for many years, but my wife and I find that we really like living in an apartment - there's so much less to care for." "I'd be glad to teach your children to swim." "The schools are so convenient." "They have special movies for children each Saturday at the neighborhood theatre."

Give a bit of yourself each time you return a remark. "I used to have a dog. Had her for sixteen years and just never have been able to replace her with another animal." "It's real nice being a grandfather - all the pleasure without the responsibility." And smile. "We've lived in this area for five years and just love it here." And smile.

Practice this kind of rapport with your friends and acquaintances. The next time you go to your barber see what you can find out about him, be genuinely interested in what he says and listen well. Always return his answer with some little bit of yourself, smile and ask another question. When you drop bits of information concerning yourself, it puts the other person at ease and makes him feel he is getting acquainted with you. Tenants like to feel they know their resident manager, that he is their friend and that he will help them when they need him. They like to tell their friends what a swell guy he is or how delightful his wife is. Many people have been known to stay in one apartment house for years simply because they like the resident manager, when they could go elsewhere and get as much or more, for the same or less rent. This is selling yourself, giving of yourself and being a friend.

KNOW YOUR AREA

If a resident manager has just moved into a new area, he should immediately set about knowing the area; the location of the closest grocery store or shopping district, the location of all the schools and how the children get there, two or three good doctors and dentists, how long it takes to get to downtown and what kind of transportation there is, where the churches of different denominations are located and the times of their services, where one can enjoy a Sunday afternoon picnic or do a little fishing. Keep street maps of your area to give to new tenants, and know the different school districts and which one your building is in. Know the different services offered in the various shops of the neighborhood and the general prices. Be able to tell where horses can be boarded and know the cost. The resident manager should endeavor to know as much as possible about his area and have the information at his fingertips.

SHOWING THE HOUSE AND APARTMENT

Through the years there has been building a rather mechanical method of showing the apartment house and the apartment for rent. If the resident manager simply goes through the mechanics routinely, he is showing the apartment. If at the same time he continues to sell himself and begins, now, pointing out all the strong points of his building and continues to do this throughout his showing, he is selling an apartment. Without the selling and sincere interest in his building the showing will amount to nothing.

When the prospective tenant is first met at the door of the manager's apartment, or in the office, the resident manager should smile, extend his hand and announce his full name (in preference to "Mr. Jones"), state he is the manager of the building, and invite the prospective tenant in to have a seat. The prospective tenant will usually respond with his own name and then state that he is looking for an apartment. At this point the resident manager starts selling himself. In the process of carrying on what seems to be a casual conversation, the giving to each other mutual information, the resident manager is careful to ask the questions he needs in order to best select the right apartment for his prospect; how large the prospect's family is; what price range he prefers; whether he prefers the ground floor or an upper floor, near the swimming pool or away from it. Listen carefully to all his answers and record them in your memory. Don't rush your prospective tenant but let him have time to think out and put his thoughts into words. When you feel you have enough information to make the decision on which apartment to show him, suggest that the two of you take a walk to see the grounds and facilities and the apartment you have in mind for him.

WHILE GOING TO THE APARTMENT

Always take the most attractive route available to reach the apartment. This would naturally lead past or through the pool area, recreation room, game rooms if any, and if your prospective tenant happens to be a woman, be sure to show her the laundry areas and note how convenient they are to the apartment you are going to show her. This is the time to point out the strong points of the building itself, its fine construction, how the buildings are grouped in order to insure maximum privacy for each tenant, the play yard for children and the beautiful manner in which the grounds are kept. This could be the time to talk about the nice people who live in your building and how well they care for their apartments, pets and children. The prospective tenant should be told of the company policy that helps insure quiet, peaceful comfort and of the safeguards that promote and maintain mental comfort for the residents.

IN THE APARTMENT

When you have reached the apartment you have chosen, open the door and precede the prospect into the apartment, stepping aside to allow him to enter, just as if you were opening a door to a guest. If your prospect is a woman, show the kitchen first, since that is where the woman of the family spends most of her time. Open the doors to the refrigerator, stove and cabinets to show how clean they are and reveal their size. Always stand aside and behind the doors when opening them so that your prospective tenant has an unobstructed view of the interior. If there is an unusually nice view out of a certain window, call this to his attention. Go then into the bedrooms, opening all the closet doors to call attention to their size. Open the hall closets to show the amount of storage space. Next go into the bathroom. The toilet seat and lid should be down, but not to hide a dirty toilet. Never, never show an apartment with a dirty toilet, even if it happens to be residue that has collected while the apartment has been vacant. Just as surely as you do, the prospect will open up the toilet to see for himself.

Walk casually back to the living room to take a better look at it and the dining space. Draperies in an empty apartment being shown should always be left open, unless there is some definite reason for them to be closed. In winter months having the draperies closed on entrance creates a dark and dismal entrance for the prospective tenant, and the hustling around of the resident manager opening them, and then closing them again on leaving, is a distraction. The entrance is so much nicer if the prospective tenant walks into a bright, cheerful living room. If there is a particularly striking view out of the window, so much the better. If there is the opposite, that is, a bad view from one of the windows, the draperies in this room might be kept closed if possible, though the prospective tenant will usually find a way to look out that very window. There are occasions, on hot summer days, in a building with no air conditioning, when the draperies should be closed against the heat to try to keep the apartment cooler and also to help guard against fading of carpets and furniture.

The resident manager should listen with his eyes, watching everything his prospective tenant seems most interested in examining. If he seems to be looking for dirt, point out the policy of cleanliness you and your company maintain. If it happens to be the dishwasher, note that it is supposed to be the best model that particular company ever made. Point out the plusses of your apartment that are not obvious.

OVERCOMING OBJECTIONS

Perhaps your building is not one that has a swimming pool and other niceties that many big complexes have these days. When this is noted by your prospective tenant, you should counter that the very lack of a pool is one of the reasons so many "quiet" people like to live there and call attention to the beautifully landscaped yard with lawn furniture for sunning, or just sitting and reading. Perhaps you will have a badminton court, croquet court or a fire pit for roasting hot dogs in the evening. Then tell where, and how close, the nearest swimming pool is and tell about the tennis courts, "just across the street." If your prospect complains about the lack of a dishwasher, remark that there is so much space on the counter top that a drying rack can easily be used and that not drying dishes is half the battle. After all, you cannot deny the lack of a dishwasher. These are only a few suggestions. Each resident manager should know his own building, its strong points and weak ones. He should give a great deal of thought to how he plans to overcome the weak points. He should never call attention to the weak points, to be sure, but he should be prepared to counter with constructive and cheerful remarks when the weak points are brought up and turn them more to his advantage than disadvantage. The rent structure is probably lower in a building without all the recreational facilities of the large complexes, and this is a definite advantage; however this point should always be brought out in a manner that does not disparage the prospective tenant's ability to pay.

KEEP SELLING

If your prospect appears to be sold on the apartment and ready to rent, guide him back to your apartment or office and proceed with writing up the agreements. Some remark should be made at this point to give your prospect an opportunity to either say yes or no, or that he must show his wife, or she must have her husband see the apartment. Keep talking about some of the strong points you have saved for this time, such as: "Did you notice the floor is new in the bathroom?" or "That closet in the hallway is unusually large." The resident manager should never appear overanxious, but he should always ask the prospective tenant if he would like the apartment held for him, or make some other remark equally pointed toward renting the apartment. This is called "asking for a closing" in the sales field and is considered a crucial factor in selling. Sometimes a person really is sold but is very hesitant about saying so. By asking for a closing you are giving that person an opportunity to say yes or no, or that she will have to let her husband see it first. Whatever the answer, the resident manager should never in any way try to delay his prospective tenant's departure.

SHOW A FURNISHED UNIT FOR COMPARISON

If your building is rented unfurnished and you have a model unit, always show the furnished model unit to your prospective tenant. This will help him visualize how his own furniture will look in the apartment.

NEVER ATTEMPT THE HARD SELL

If the resident manager has shown his prospective tenant his grounds and apartment and his prospective tenant definitely states that it will not do – there simply is not enough space, or he must have a swimming pool or other facility your building does not offer – do not try to change his mind. It will only antagonize him, and create ill will for you and your company. Know what kind of apartment houses are in the location he desires (your area). Hopefully your own company will have another building in the area that will fit his needs, and direct him to another, still trying to be helpful and cheerful. Thank him for allowing you to show him your building. He will remember you and your building with kindness and perhaps return your favor by sending someone around one day whose needs fit your building and facilities. And always keep smiling.

SECOND SHOWING

The resident manager has now made his first showing. He has gathered all the information for his traffic report and he has given his prospective tenant an opportunity to rent the apartment at this time. It is very seldom that an unfurnished apartment is rented to a couple, with or without children, on the first showing if it is shown to only one member of the couple. Suppose your prospective tenant is a woman and she has stated she likes the apartment but must bring her husband to see it before she can rent it. Maybe she would like to come around early in the morning, before her husband goes to work. The resident manager could promise a cup of fresh coffee and a sweet roll; in the evening, perhaps a cup of tea or a glass of lemonade. He should press for a specified time for the second showing.

When the husband is brought in, the resident manager should sort of turn the selling job over to his prospective tenant, as it is obvious that she would not have brought her husband to see the apartment if she herself were not sold. She has been telling him about it and now she herself wants to show him all the features she likes so well. Also, she is better able to know his objections and how to overcome them than is the resident manager. The manager should maintain a courteous silence, answer any questions that may be asked and supply additional information that the wife may have forgotten or overlooked.

BACK IN THE OFFICE

By now the resident manager has either rented or not rented the apartment, but let us assume here that he has rented it. Now he carefully guides the tenants-to-be through the application for rental, the lease or rental agreement, the pet deposit and authorization, if any. He explains the key deposit and mail. He again calls to their attention company policy concerning pets, children, etc. After the rental agreement has been signed, he calls attention to the rules and regulations enforced in his building, explains fully the state laws concerning vacating notice, refunding of deposit and other things the tenant must know. Absolutely nothing will save misunderstandings and ill feelings between the resident manager and tenant so much as will a full explanation in the beginning. The resident manager has probably already mentioned many of these things in the process of showing the apartment, but at this time it is very wise indeed to cover everything again in a very explanatory manner. And keep right on smiling!

CHAPTER VIII

HOW TO CLEAN AN APARTMENT

There is nothing more important to renting an apartment than spotless cleanliness. Every speck of dirt, however remote, must be removed from the vacant apartment before it is shown to a prospective tenant. A woman will put up with small inconveniences to live in an apartment of her choice, but she will not clean up dirt and grime left by a former tenant. The kitchen and bathroom must not only look and smell clean and sanitary, they must be clean and sanitary.

A small maid's cart can be a handy item around an apartment house. All cleaning supplies – brooms, mops, vacuum cleaners, cleansers, cloths, and disinfectants – can be carried and moved around on a maid's cart. A cart like a grocery cart can be used. Even a basket will help a lot in carrying small items. Or just fix up a sturdy cardboard box with a rope handle.

CARRY OUT TRASH AND FORGOTTEN ITEMS

Check the entire apartment for items forgotten and trash. Put them all into one big box. Turn the refrigerator off when checking it and remove anything that might have been left. Empty the ice trays and refill them with hot water to start the defrosting. When looking for trash, be sure to pull the lower drawers of the cabinets in the kitchen completely out to see if anything has fallen beneath them. Pull the stove drawer completely out to check the drawer and the space below it. Open the dishwasher and check below the water fan for broken glass, measuring spoons or cups. Check the garbage disposal; let it run to do away with any residual garbage and remove anything that may not grind up. Using a stepladder check to the very back corner of all of the upper cabinets for items that may have been missed. Open and check every drawer and cabinet in the kitchen. Open and check all storage closets, drawers and shelves in the entire apartment and remove every last item found. Remove all that is found to the garbage containers.

USE THE VACUUM CLEANER

Use the vacuum cleaner to remove all loose dirt in the apartment. Clean the kitchen cabinets inside and out with the vacuum. With the wall brush and dusting brush, clean the walls, tops of draperies, tops of drapery rods, heaters, light fixtures, switch and plug plates, shelves, cabinets and drawers. Make a habit of looking up to the ceiling at all the corners for cobwebs and down to the floor for dirt. Keep looking for small edges that might catch dirt. Vacuum all you can out of the slides of sliding doors and windows. Don't forget the hall closets and bathroom cabinets. While doing the vacuuming, make a mental note of all areas that may need spot cleaning on the walls. Vacuum all floors and carpets thoroughly.

DON'T TRACK DIRT IN FROM OUTSIDE

Sweep and clean all deck and lanai areas thoroughly so as not to track dirt back into the apartment you are cleaning. This includes the area in front of the entrance. All dirt and trash should have been carried to the trashcans. If there is a storage closet on the deck or lanai, be sure to open it and carry out anything that might have been left there and clean all dirt and cobwebs out of it.

WINDOWS

Any mildew on the window sash must be removed with chlorine bleach and an old toothbrush after scraping as much as possible out with a blunt instrument. If the bleach doesn't remove all of it, it must be cleaned out with steel wool. After it is clean, wipe it out with a solution of household ammonia to hold down further mildewing. I am speaking here of aluminum sash. If you have painted wooden sash, clean it as you would any other woodwork. If it is badly mildewed, it may need a new coat of paint. If you can reach both sides of the window, clean and polish both sides. If there are specks of paint on the windows, this is the time to take it off with a single-edged razor blade in a holder. If you don't have any rags, buy some cheesecloth.

WALLS

If there are nails in the walls, carefully remove them. If there are small picture hangers, leave them; the new tenant may be able to use them. If there are stick-on picture hangers on the walls, they should not be removed unless the apartment is definitely scheduled for painting, as they tear the paint off the wall when removed.

There will likely be dirty smudges around the light switches and plug plates; shoe marks along the top of the baseboard and hand marks around corners at the points of the heaviest traffic. If the switch plates and plug plates are quite dirty, remove them and wash them in warm sudsy water. Before replacing them, try cleaning the wall around them with a good spray cleaner. Spot clean the walls in all the rooms with the spray cleaner. While letting the cleaner sit for the few seconds it takes to work, keep the rivulets wiped back up into the wet spot. Wipe the area with a damp cloth or sponge, feathering out the edges. If there are large areas of dark smudges above the heaters, the apartment probably will need painting. However, the spot cleaning should be done anyway, as it is possible that only one or two walls in each room will actually need painting.

The small black marks at the bottom of the wall, where the toes of shoes may have hit, can quite often be removed with the tiniest bit of scouring powder on a damp cloth over the end of your finger. Be very careful to rub lightly and only on the spots: heavy rubbing may remove the paint. Unless an apartment has been misused and not kept up by the tenant, a paint job should last at least one year and with careful tenants can last two and three years. Be certain the walls look as if they had been painted when you have the apartment ready to show. If they do not, they should be painted.

CHECK EVERY SMALL ITEM

Check the tops of drapery rods, thermostats, baseboards, all corners, and wipe clean with a rag dampened with warm sudsy water or spray cleaner. Remove the bowls from the light fixtures, clean out dust and bugs, and wash and polish the bowls before replacing. This is the time to check and replace any burned-out light bulbs. If there are chandelier type fixtures, or fixtures finished in brass, wipe clean with a damp cloth and polish with a dry clean cloth. Anything in the entire apartment that can shine should be polished.

CARPETS

The most important part of shampooing a carpet is the vacuuming before shampooing. If shampoo is put on a dirty carpet (that is, full of dust), it will turn out muddy and can stain the carpet. If you are required to do the carpet shampooing by your company, you should be furnished with equipment for this purpose and a good heavy-duty vacuum cleaner. Your company will have equipment and supply of the type they prefer and should have complete directions for you. Follow their instructions to the letter. Some companies prefer to send someone in to do the job. If there are small areas of dirt which the vacuum did not remove, try spot-cleaning with a good carpet cleaner. You may save your company the cost of cleaning one carpet.

Sometimes you will find small burn holes in carpets where a cinder or cigarette has been dropped. Small holes, not more than two inches in diameter, can be repaired by trimming away the burned nap down to the bottom of the carpet, then cutting a matching piece out of a closet. A lot of apartment houses will have pieces of carpet stored for just this purpose. Trim away the heaviest part of the burlap backing on the piece you plan to use for your patch, being careful not to reach the nap and separate it, then glue it into the trimmed hole in the carpet with good contact cement. Shag rugs with a rather long nap can often have the top part of the nap trimmed if the burn has not gone deep. On a shag rug with an uneven texture this will never be seen. A carpet repairman should repair any damage larger than two to three inches in diameter. Any tears or separated seams should be reported so that your company can send out a repairman.

HARDWOOD FLOORS

Hardwood floors should be cleaned with a good wax stripper, then re-waxed and polished with a floor buffer. If you have hardwood floors to care for, your company will probably have all the equipment and supply you will need for your work and will give you instructions on their use. When re-waxing any floor, hold the wax back from the baseboard just a little so as not to build up a heavy coating of wax at the edge where there is no traffic. If you have hardwood floors to care for, it is a good idea to cover the traffic areas with strips of paper while showing the apartment.

BATHROOM

Always carry one or two large, clean, dry cloths with you for polishing the mirrors and all the chrome and for drying out the fixtures after they have been cleaned. *Bathtub.* The walls, regardless of the type of material used, above the tub or around the shower stalls should be scrubbed with soapy water containing disinfectant, rinsed, and wiped dry. If ceramic or plastic tile has been installed, it must be cleaned with either scouring powder or one of the tile cleaners on the market. All the grout - plaster joints between the tiles and around the tub - should be scrubbed with a brush to remove every bit of soap scum that collects there. If these joints show a brownish tinge, it is likely there is soap scum left on them. Use a small brush, such as an old toothbrush, to get into the corners. If the grout is broken out around the tub, it should be reported to your company so they can send a repairman out. When cleaning the chrome fixtures, always use a very wet and sudsy solution of the scouring powder, then rinse well. If chrome fixtures are cleaned with dry scouring powder, or wet powder is allowed to dry on the fixture before polishing, it will scratch the surface and can eventually dull or even wear off the chrome. Soap scum and dirt collects around the edges of all fixtures. Be sure this is cleaned out so one cannot see any ring of dirt around the fixture edges. Use your fingernails, toothpick or orange stick if it cannot be removed any other way. If there is a removable plug in the drain, remove it; clean down the drain as far as you can reach with your finger or a bottle brush. If the drain seems sluggish, plunge it out with a plunger. Don't forget to clean inside as far as you can reach in the overflow drain. Always rinse all areas well and then dry with a polishing cloth. Don't let water stand in any of the porcelain, as it leaves water spots. Dry and polish all chrome fixtures and mirrors.

Lavatory. Clean the entire area with scouring powder. Remove the drain if possible and clean. Clean down the drain as far as possible with your finger or bottlebrush. Clean every edge where chrome meets porcelain, or metal meets porcelain, or formica with a small brush, your fingernails or small pointed stick. Don't forget the overflow drain. Rinse all areas well; dry and polish all chrome and porcelain. If you have a lavatory without a cabinet built around it, be sure not to neglect the outside and underneath. Get down under the lavatory so you can see up under it and clean all areas you can reach, including the walls under and around it. Clean and polish the valves and water pipes leading to the lavatory and the drainpipe going from it. These should be cleaned when they are enclosed in a cabinet also. If there is a sticky residue on the formica around a lavatory remove it with a sudsy solution of the scouring powder or one of the spray cleaners. Always rinse well and dry.

Toilet. There is only one way to properly clean a toilet. That is to get your hands into it and scrub. While this is repugnant to many people, the use of rubber gloves makes it much less so. An unusually dirty toilet bowl can be cleaned with some disinfectant and bowl brush first and then you won't feel so bad about putting your hands into it. The water in the bowl should be pushed down the drain with the cleaning cloth as much as possible, then sprinkle the entire surface with scouring powder and scrub; up under the edge where the water comes in, in the small hole the water comes in, and down the drain as far as you can reach. The little holes up under the edge of the toilet can get plugged with residue from the water and sometimes even impair the efficient operation of the toilet. Look at them with a little hand mirror to see if they are clean and open. Clean the upper edge of the toilet bowl with a sudsy solution of the scouring powder, being sure to get under the back part of the seat where it is connected to the bowl. Use a toothbrush to get every bit of dirt out of the edges of the connection and clean the back part of the bowl behind the seat. Clean the seat and lid in the same manner, being sure there is no line of residue around any of the rubber bumpers on the bottom of the seat. This is the time to replace any bumpers on the bottom of the seat that are worn. Remove the lid to the water tank and clean the entire exterior of the water tank and toilet bowl with a sudsy solution of scouring powder. Don't neglect the bottom of the water tank and the backside of the toilet bowl. Underneath the water tank is a water pipe to the water tank with a valve on it. This is usually made of chrome-plated metal and is the most neglected of all cleaning in the bathroom. Clean and polish it and wipe the walls down behind and all around the toilet and water tank. While you have the lid off the water tank, check to see how much residue is on the inside walls of the tank. In some areas the water carries much residue that attaches itself to the inside walls of the water tank; if this is removed occasionally, the toilet bowl will stay clean longer. Use a long slim brush similar to a bottlebrush and brush the sides of the tank down while flushing the toilet. Be careful not to damage any of the plumbing inside the tank. Water tanks in some areas of the country can have almost a half-inch of mud in the bottom that has collected over a period of years. This should be washed down periodically. Be sure to clean all areas of the toilet and water tank, which you cannot see. Rinse all areas well, dry and polish.

On the bottom edge of the toilet bowl, where it sits on the floor the plumbers use a putty – a "seating compound." This is used to seal the seam, to keep moisture from running under the bowl onto the sub floor that would eventually cause rotting of the sub floor. Sometimes as an apartment is lived in there is a compressing of this and some of it will be sticking out around the edge of the bottom of the bowl. This causes an unsightly joint and is a collection point for dirt -and germs. This should not be pulled out but should be cut off even with the bottom of the fixture, and the floor cleaned up to it. In an older building this seal may have become hard and brittle and have holes in it. If it can be patched, it should be. Sometimes it is necessary to pull the fixture and reset it with new compound. If it has gone this far, probably the seal ring around the drainpipe is gone too and needs replacing.

Medicine cabinet. Medicine cabinets should be cleaned with a sudsy solution of scouring powder, rinsed and dried. If they are wooden and the shelves will not come out and stains will not come off, then repaint them with a good grade of white enamel. If they are metal and the shelves are removable, remove them and scour the interior. If the entire interior is stained, repaint. If only the floor of the cabinet is rusted, it can be covered with plastic adhesive shelf paper, applied very neatly.

Floor. Special attention should be given to the corners and joints around the edges of the floor. After removing the old wax with a good stripper get down and clean all the corners with a cloth. Rinse the floor and dry well before applying new wax. Use a good grade of liquid wax or the kind your company supplies. Again, hold the wax back about an inch from the edge to avoid build-up.

Touch-up Paint for Porcelain: All of the porcelain fixtures in an apartment are likely to, at one time or another, get chipped by something heavy falling into them. If these chips are not too large, they can be covered with a good grade of retouching enamel made for the purpose. When touching up nicks in porcelain, it is always best to use several layers of thin enamel in order to create a build-up more even with the surface. With experience it can even be rubbed down with a polishing compound, and then the patched spot is hardly seen.

KITCHEN

Cabinets. Clean all kitchen cabinets, inside and out, with your favorite brand of cleaner or one furnished by your company. Don't forget the inside of cabinet doors. If adhesive plastic-coated paper has been neatly applied to the shelves, it is better to clean it and leave it there; sometimes it is a mess to try to remove, and the surface is very durable. Small nicks or scratches on dark wooden doors can be hidden by rubbing a little dark stain into them. Ordinary furniture polish will liven up dull woodwork, or use one of the new cleaners on the market made especially for woodwork.

Refrigerator. Spray the oven in the stove so it will be ready to clean when you are through with the refrigerator. By now the refrigerator should be defrosted and cleaning shouldn't be too much of a problem. All removable shelves and trays should be removed and cleaned separately before replacing. Clean the interior with a solution of baking soda in hot water, dry and replace shelves. If there are spills that detergent and soap will not remove, try a small amount of scouring powder and clean only on the spots. Be sure to get into all corners and clean all seams and crevices. Clean well around the hinges and into the screw heads that are exposed. Replace the ice trays empty, and turn the refrigerator on low. Pull the refrigerator away from the wall so you can clean the wall and floor behind and under it. Before replacing the refrigerator, clean the exterior, rinse and dry with a clean cloth. A dull surface can be polished with a good grade of appliance polish. If there is dirt and grime in and around the hinge connection or the emblem, use a toothbrush and scrub it out. Remove the grill from the lower part of the refrigerator and vacuum as much as you can of the collected dust from the under part of the box and fins, if any. While you are there, check the drip tray for cleanliness and remove it and wash it if necessary. Don't forget the rubber gasket around the refrigerator door. Sometimes this is sort of in pleats and must be separated so it can be cleaned inside. On dark smudges that can't be removed with a damp cloth, use a little scouring powder.

Stove Oven. You should have removed elements that are removable before spraying. If there happen to be chrome drip trays under the top burners of the stove you are cleaning, they can be put into the oven along with the chrome shelves before spraying. Use a good grade of oven cleaner and spray the entire surface, being careful not to overload the elements. The oven should stand at least twenty minutes. Use paper towels when cleaning a stove. If the oven isn't too dirty, one spraying should be enough. After removal of as much of the cleaner as possible with paper towels, wipe the entire interior surface of the oven and door several times with a sponge or wet rag to remove all traces of the cleaner. Be sure to wipe the elements clean of the oven cleaner. If there are black burned-on grease spots that the cleaner has not removed, go over the entire surface of the oven with a stainless-steel sponge. (This is not steel wool. There are several brands of these stainless-steel sponges on the market.) Use a lot of elbow grease. Every black speck and spot can and should be removed from the surface of the oven. If the stainless-steel sponge doesn't remove them all, use a razor-blade scraper. If there is still a problem spot that has been there for years, use medium to coarse sandpaper. All of this work is done dry, that is, without water; it works better and is cleaner and faster.

The chrome shelves should have come fairly clean with the oven-cleaner. Finish them up with the stainless- steel sponge and steel-wool soap pad. Dry and polish and replace in the oven. Never let a commercial oven cleaner stand in an oven overnight or long enough to dry on the surface, as this can do permanent damage to the elements and interior walls of the oven.

If you are cleaning a stove with a self-cleaning oven do not clean the oven with the chrome oven trays or put the chrome drip pans in the oven. The heat in the oven while cleaning will burn the chrome off the metal. Be sure to follow the instructions that came with the stove.

Stove Top. Remove all drip trays, and removable parts from the top of the stove. If you have chrome drip trays, they should have come fairly clean with the oven spray. If you have chrome rings that are removable around the burners, they can also be put in the oven with the spray cleaner on them. You can finish them with the stainless-steel sponge and steel-wool soap pad. If you have soft-aluminum drip trays, it has always been assumed that practically anything you put on them to soak will turn their color or dull their surface. The usual method of cleaning these has been to soak them in detergent and then scrub them first with the stainless-steel sponge (which scratches a little but works well under water), and then with steel-wool soap pads and they will come clean and shiny. But it isn't easy; it takes a lot of hard scrubbing.

There are aluminum cleaners on the market that make this job a lot easier. Since they are very toxic, one should use rubber gloves while handling them. In a well-ventilated area, such as a garage or carport, apply and leave on for twenty minutes to an hour. When the cleaner is rinsed off, there will be a residue of the burned grease left, but it is dry and flaky and a swish or two with the stainless-steel sponge removes it. There will be some stain left, but a steel-wool soap pad will remove it in less than a minute per tray. These cleaners are expensive (about a dollar for five ounces, retail) but five ounces should clean four drip trays at least twice. Companies should supply this cleaner to their resident managers who have to clean aluminum drip trays and broilers; it would save them many dollars in labor.

All of the little knobs on a stove will slip off for cleaning and you can clean under them. Do not soak them if they have painted-on numbers or letters; soaking, even for a short period, will remove that paint. You can clean them a with a little brush and get all of the grease out of the creases and crevices that manufacturers seem to love to put into stoves just to catch the grease. Clean underneath the burners with the stainless-steel sponge, if necessary, being sure to reach all the way back into the corners. Wipe clean and dry. The chrome rings on the stove burners come amazingly clean with just the stainless-steel sponge. Be sure to clean the edges of the rings and under them. The edge around the burner and where the drip trays sit can be cleaned with the stainless-steel sponge. Dry and polish the whole surface of the stove. Every bit of chrome on the stove should shine like a mirror. If you have a set-in stove instead of a drop-in unit or built-in unit, you then have dirty sides on the stove and dirty sides on the cabinets where it sits The stove should be pulled, the floors and walls all cleaned and replaced. The exterior of the entire stove should be cleaned, and all surfaces dried and polished with a clean dry cloth. Every edge where chrome meets porcelain or formica should have been cleaned out with the fingernails or a sharp-pointed instrument of some kind so there is no ring of dirt or grease left there.

Nicks in the stove or refrigerator can be filled with touch-up paint. Remember that touch-up paint will shortly turn brown on the stove, as it will not stand up under the heat. The touch-up paint will last long enough for you to rent the apartment, and if requested, you can always add more if necessary. It takes very little time, and you will have pleased a tenant.

Dishwashers. Dishwashers are often neglected. Because dishes are washed in them every day, one thinks of them as clean. This, of course, is not true. There are bits of food in the strainers, and residue of water and dishwasher detergent on the entire interior. The shelves should be removed and the interior cleaned with a sudsy solution of scouring powder. The strainers should be removed and polished. After cleaning, the dishwasher should be put through one complete cycle without detergent and then dried out. The dishwasher should then be left open so it dries inside.

.*Garbage disposals*. The inside of the garbage disposal collects all kinds of dirt, grease and food residue. It is not necessary for them to look black and rusty. If they are cleaned out with scouring powder, even once a week, they will never get black and dirty looking. If they are left in this dirty condition, the blades and moving parts will rust and stick and they will have to be broken loose by forcing the blade to turn. The resident manger should always clean the garbage disposal with a brush and scouring powder if his hand will not go into it. If he can get his hand into it, he can reach up under the edge where brushes are likely not to reach. It should be run several minutes to rinse and then dried out to the best of your ability. If the apartment is vacant for a long period, the garbage disposal should be started and run several minutes each week.

Floor. The kitchen floor should be stripped of old wax with a good wax stripper and rinsed well and a new coat of liquid wax applied. Be sure to get down on the floor to clean out all corners, and check the condition of the baseboard. Sometimes the baseboard has had most of its finish taken off with frequent mopping; a new coat of varnish or paint will make it like new.

DRAINS

When drains clog up, it is usually from accumulations of normal waste materials. In the kitchen these are grease and food residue; in the bathtub, soap scum and hair. If the toilet gets plugged up, nine out of ten times some object has been dropped into it. Most drain problems can be solved with the use of the rubber plunger and flushing the drain with hot water. There are times when a drain has not been cleaned for so long that the residue in the trap has become hard and the plunger will not move it. In this case one might need to get a plumber's snake to run through the drain several times. If this does not unplug the drain, the trouble is probably farther down in the drain and a plumber will have to be called. If the toilet is plugged up and the plunger will not pull anything from it, and it cannot be reached with the hand, the resident manager should call the company for help because it is likely the toilet will have to be pulled and reset to find the trouble. If women could be taught to run the hottest water in the tap down drains for two minutes each week, that would eliminate much stoppage of kitchen and bathroom drains.

SHINE, SHINE, SHINE

A lot has been said about making everything shine and always carrying a clean, dry polishing cloth. There are two reasons for this: First, if it shines it has to be clean. Second, everything that has a shiny, polished surface will catch the eye when the apartment is shown, and any small imperfections may be overlooked. A shiny-clean bathroom and kitchen are the greatest assets to any apartment. They must be clean enough for the most particular person to use without hesitation.

FURNISHED APARTMENTS

The furnished apartment has the additional problem of furniture cleaning. All upholstered pieces should have cushions removed and must be vacuumed inside and out. If there is obvious dirt, the upholstery will have to be cleaned with upholstery cleaner. If there are slip- covers, they should be washed or dry cleaned and replaced. If there are rips or tears in the upholstery, they should be repaired if possible. If not possible, perhaps slip covering is the answer; or the company might have the furniture reupholstered. The varnished wooden parts should all be cleaned and polished with furniture polish. Scratches on dark wood can be hidden by rubbing a little stain into them. Painted furniture should always be washed and dried. Sometimes an old table can look mighty good with a new coat of paint, and then you know it is clean. If mattresses have been stained, they should be sent out to be cleaned and disinfected. The resident manager should always endeavor to keep a good mattress pad on the mattresses of a furnished apartment. If contour pads with waterproof backing were furnished, companies would find that mattresses would last longer. They could be taken off and washed each time there was a change of tenancy.

CHECKING VACANCIES

After the apartment is completely cleaned and ready to show, go back to it at least once a week to check it until it is rented. Carry a cloth to dust with, flush the toilet and check it for a water ring. If there is one, remove it. Check the refrigerator for odor. Run the garbage disposal for a few minutes. Be sure there is no water standing in the dishwasher. Check the entrances for dirt and dust that might have collected since you cleaned the apartment and remove it.

CHAPTER IX

MAINTENANCE OF PUBLIC SPACES

Keeping the exterior of your apartment building clean and neat at all times is part of the resident manager's job. All parts of the building the public has access to are called public spaces. This includes recreation rooms, game rooms, saunas, exercise rooms, swimming pools, wading pools, exterior decks, interior halls, elevators, storage areas, laundry rooms, children's play areas, sidewalks, driveways, lawns and planted areas. All these areas must be watched and inspected daily. The resident manger should make a habit of picking up any piece of paper or trash as he sees it. The atmosphere of the building is created by the cleanliness and care of the public spaces. If the resident manager puts forth a real effort to care for his public spaces, he can usually count on the tenants' cooperation.

LAUNDRY ROOMS

If you are in a large, spread out complex, the laundry rooms in your building may be numerous, rather small and spaced to give greater convenience to the tenant. If your building is small and compact, you may have only one laundry room to tend. Most modern buildings have coin-operated, automatic washing machines and dryers that are owned, installed and maintained by an outside company which does nothing else. If you have repair problems with the laundry equipment, you will have a number to call the company directly for service. Always keep a trash container in the laundry room. All laundry rooms must be inspected once a day. At that time, the dryers should be checked for lint and removed. Carry a damp cloth to wipe the exterior of the equipment and clean the top of the washing machine around the drum and at the top and around the hinges of the lid. Pick up any trash or lint on the floor and empty the trash containers at least two or three times a week. If the floor looks dirty, clean it even it if has been cleaned the day before. If your building keeps bulletin boards in the laundry rooms, check for outdated notices and remove them. If you are in a large building with numerous laundry rooms, there will probably be an assistant manager to take care of some of this work, but it is your job to see that he does it properly.

RECREATION ROOMS, SAUNAS, GAME ROOMS, ETC.

Recreation rooms are public places in that they are for the tenant's use. They are reserved by the tenant for his use on a particular date. He will either pay a fee for the use of it or make a deposit that will be returned to him after the resident manager has inspected the room to see that it has been cleaned to the company's specifications. Recreation rooms are for the tenants' use at times other than when they may be reserved for a private party. They often have card tables or other recreational facilities and fireplaces. Tenants may use them for impromptu card games, just conversation, or having a drink or cup of coffee while watching the children play in the pool. Consequently, they must be checked frequently, the ashtrays emptied, things picked up, etc. One might say the recreation room is the apartment's living room; so it must always be ready for guests. It is the resident manager's duty to keep records of reservations, post notices for those dates and see that the recreation room is in order. It will occasionally need to have windows cleaned and polished and the floor cleaned and waxed. Recreation rooms usually have vinyl floors since water can be tracked from the pool and so that the tenants may have dancing parties.

Saunas, exercise rooms and game rooms should all be checked daily. Ashtrays should be emptied, and cleaned if needed. Saunas should be cleaned with disinfectant twice a week. Exercise equipment should be checked frequently to be sure it is in good running order. Game equipment, such as cards or darts and billiard equipment, should be continually watched. Card decks with lost or torn cards should be replaced, and cues should be repaired or replaced as needed. Game rooms and exercise rooms are of no use to tenants if the equipment furnished is out of order.

GARBAGE AREAS

The garbage areas should be checked daily, any trash around picked up and put in the container and the lids closed. If you find the lids are not being closed by tenants, post a courteous sign requesting it. If you find your containers are not holding all the trash between pickups, let your company know about it so you can get additional space. Lids should be kept closed at all times to avoid odor and flies.

CHILDREN'S PLAY YARDS

There should never be a broken or damaged piece of equipment left in a children's play area. This might cause an injury to a child and it would be a liability to both you and your company. If there is broken equipment and it cannot be repaired or replaced, remove it and store it, or with permission from your company give it to a charitable institution. The play areas should be checked daily. All small articles or bits of glass or metal should be removed immediately. Sandboxes should be covered each night with canvas or wire to keep cats out. Check the latches on the gates to be sure small children cannot open them, and repair them if necessary.

DECKS, SIDEWALKS, DRIVEWAYS

All decks, sidewalks, and driveways should be kept free of dirt, trash and leaves. They should be swept and washed down with water periodically. Grease spots should be removed from the driveways, as they build up and gather dirt. Your company will probably supply you with a grease remover. The choice of time in cleaning sidewalks and decks is important. The manager should try not to disturb sleeping children but should do this cleaning when the tenants are likely to see him. This will bring it to their attention that you are trying to keep things clean and the manager will get more cooperation from the tenants.

If your building is a compact building with interior hallways and stairs or elevators, the hallways should be vacuumed two or three times a week and the entrance to the building kept clean each day. Cigarette receptacles should be emptied each day. Attention should be given to the ceilings and corners to see that they are not collecting cobwebs. Stairways should be kept clean and free of trash and any wooden surfaces or rails should be dusted often.

LAWNS

A lawn should never be cut shorter than one and one-half inches. Cut grass should not be left on the lawn. If there are a few weeds in the grass, they should be pulled or cut out and bare areas reseeded. If there are a lot of weeds, a good selective weed killer should be used. The lawn should be fertilized each year to insure a good healthy color and tight growth. At all edges where the lawn abuts a driveway, sidewalk or planted area there should be an edging process, and the grass neatly trimmed. The edge should not be more than two inches deep and one inch wide, but this will allow water to run off the drive or walk and make washing walks and driveways easier. Grass should always be well trimmed around planted areas so it doesn't get tangled up with the plants and choke them. Your lawn should always be free of leaves, rubbish and animal droppings.

PLANTED AREAS

The planted areas should always be kept free of leaves and trash and the surface kept raked and smooth. Pull weeds out as you walk around on your daily inspection. If you live in an area where a lot of mulch is used in planting areas, keep the mulch pulled uphill a little from the lawn or sidewalk and driveway edges. This keeps the mulch from running down into the lawn or onto the sidewalk. Spent summer flowers should be cut back and the areas cleaned. Annuals should not be allowed to grow wild; keep them confined to their own area. Plants of all kinds need pruning, watering and fertilizing. They also become infested with aphids and other pests so spraying with proper insecticide is necessary. Dead trees and shrubs should be removed and replaced if necessary. If you have a large tree that is dead, you should notify your company and ask for help.

PRUNING

All trees and shrubs need pruning once in a while. Large trees in a yard should be pruned high up the trunk and any dead branches removed. A tree has one leader limb, which is the extension of the trunk. This leader should never be taken out unless the tree is under electric wires, the eaves of a house or some other obstruction, which might impair its growth. A tree will strive to reach its own height. If the leader is cut, the tree will tend to grow bushy and instead of a nice strong central trunk it will grow numerous small limbs that are weak and will break in strong winds. Also, the wind blows against a bushy tree instead of through it and is much more likely to blow it over. Broad-leaved trees should be pruned for shape and area, and dead branches taken out. Evergreens should be pruned for shape. Shrubs should be controlled for the shape and area in which they are planted. A newly planted sapling should be watched carefully the first few years and not allowed to "crouch."

SWIMMING POOLS

Checking, Policing and Control. Swimming pools need constant attention, especially in summer when in use. The water should be tested for acid and chlorine content twice a day – in the morning, and the necessary chemicals added to balance the water, and again in the late afternoon after being used. The deck area should be policed each morning, ashtrays emptied, belongings left behind picked up and the deck washed down with the hose. Any tile trim should be scrubbed at least once a week. Strict regulations should be laid down for pool use, and the manager should see that these rules are followed, always being firm, explanatory and courteous. No kind of glass container should be allowed in the pool area. If a tenant wants to take a drink to the pool area, he should use a plastic container. The pool area should be continually watched when it is in use. Roughhousing children or adults should be expelled.

Algae and Colored Water. If you should have a green algae problem, it can usually be remedied by adding chlorine. For black or red algae, you may need some special help. Black and red algae attach themselves to the surface of the pool and usually need severe treatment to completely remove them. The use of algaecides, according to directions, is a good preventive measure. Report any signs of black or red algae to your company and ask for their recommendations. Small patches of black or red algae can be removed with a wire brush, but not if your pool has been painted.

Another startling thing that sometimes happens to swimming pools is that the water turns color during a period of a couple of hours. You may have a sparkling clear pool in the morning of a hot day, and within two or three hours it will turn green, blue, red or black. If this should happen, call your company immediately, as you will probably need professional help. In both cases - algae and colored water - it sometimes is easier to empty the swimming pool, thoroughly clean it, and fill it with fresh water. However *do not ever empty your swimming pool without express permission from your company*. There are areas with a high water table. If a pool in this kind of area is emptied without pumping the water out from underneath it during the time it is empty, the pool can actually be pushed up out of the ground. Any time there is this big a maintenance problem your company should give you professional help.

Skimmers. There are small holes in the top edge of the swimming pool, just under the coping, where a small part of the surface water is running out during the proper operation of the filter system. These are called skimmers and are for the purpose of taking leaves and bugs off the surface of the water before they have a chance to sink. On the deck there will be a lid that can be removed and underneath will be a strainer that catches all the debris being pulled off the water. These skimmer strainers should be checked once or twice a day and emptied if necessary.

Water Temperature. Check the temperature of the water in the pool at least twice a day and try to maintain a constant temperature. If the sun is hot in the summer, reduce the temperature to 75 degrees. If the weather is cloudy and cool, keep the temperature around 80 degrees. Young people like cooler water, but older, less active people want it just a little warmer. Never let the water in your pool get so warm that it ceases to be refreshing. There are many areas in which water must be pumped out and cold water added to bring the temperature of the water down. In these areas the swimming pool heater sometimes isn't used.

Filter Room. Constant attention should be given to the gauges on the filter. The filter equipment should be in operation twenty-four hours a day. The first sign of trouble will usually show up in the backpressure gauge. Check the backpressure gauge on the filter tanks three or four times a day and one last time before retiring. Check the tanks for air, and clean the pump strainer each day. Filters should be back-washed at least once a week; earth filters need new earth every four to six weeks. If you are using some kind of dry chlorine, do not allow smoking in the filter room, as dry chlorine is explosive. If you have a gas chlorinator and use bottled chlorine, keep a bottle of household ammonia in the filter room to detect leaks and pour if there is an accident.

GENERAL MAINTENANCE

Every resident manager should know how to change washers on faucets. He should know how to replace a plug-in or a light switch. A resident manager should build himself a small tool collection that he can carry around with him in a toolbox on service calls. A regular checking for burned-out light bulbs should be on your daily schedule. The lack of a light bulb in a stairwell could very possibly cause injury to a tenant.

It is important that you know as much as possible about your particular kind of heating system. When the service man comes to check the system, ask him a lot of questions and learn the little idiosyncrasies of your system so that you will have fewer "educational" service calls.

GETTING HELP AND INFORMATION

If you have a swimming pool to take care of and have never done this before, go to a dealer in pool equipment and supply and ask for help and pamphlets in learning how to use your particular equipment. Go to the library and look for garden books, handy-man books to study on what is needed and how to do it. Ask your furnace or air-conditioner men for information on the systems in your apartment house so you may know how they should be cared for. If you learn all these things, you will save your company many hours in labor.

Set up a routine for all the jobs that have to be done, do them without fail, and you will be running an apartment house that tenants will be proud to live in and want to bring their friends to visit.

CHAPER X

SOME THINGS TO THINK ABOUT

ABOUT YOURSELF

Are your shoes shined? Is your hair well cared for? Are your clothes neat and clean? Are your nails neatly clipped and filed? Personal appearance is a major part of any job that requires meeting the public. Are you habitually pleasant? Do you act cheerful? Are you enthusiastic about your apartment house? Do you earnestly strive not to offend anyone by word or deed? Are you friendly without being intimate?

The resident manager must be able to answer yes to all these questions, or he will fail, because he will be dealing with people. To deal with people one must understand people. We all know people who have nothing but a critical word for their fellow men. That will not work in the business of resident managership. Do you have the ability to listen? Are you a fast thinker and a slow talker? All the most successful resident mangers have been fast thinkers, fine listeners, and slow talkers. Do you have patience? Can you wait until your prospect has time to move mentally into the apartment you are showing? Do you speak with authority and knowledge about your apartment house: Are you honest? Never tell a prospective tenant anything about your house or the neighborhood that you know to be untrue. Managing an apartment house is much like having a large home with guests every night. The resident manager must see to their wants and comfort with a pleasant, happy attitude.

Do you like and respect your company? Can you honestly and sincerely report the aims and goals of your company? A resident manager must never talk with disrespect about his company or its employees. If you do not like and respect the company you are working for, you should seek other employment. Being a good resident manager is being a good public-relations person. If you sincerely feel at one with the people and the world around you, if you truly are concerned and care, if you can honestly give of yourself without feeling imposed upon, then you will be a good public-relations person; and if you are a good public-relations person, you will be a good resident manager.

ABOUT YOUR COMPANY

It is vital to the resident manager that he works with a company he respects. The manager should ask himself some questions about any company he is about to work for: Does the company have a simple but full and clear contract that sets out its policies on hiring and the terms under which the contract can be terminated by the company or the resident manager? It is always wise to know where you stand in your employment. Does the company have a written policy concerning as many situations as possible that you are apt to encounter and that you should read and subscribe to? Will you be adequately paid? Accepting employment at subnormal pay not only belittles you but also jeopardizes all others who seek or are in the same kind of employment. Are you provided with sufficient time off? Every employee, regardless of the type of work, should have reasonable free time away from his work, and it is the company's duty to see that this time is given to the resident manager without his losing money and without the apartment house being left unattended. Does the company have a training program that will start immediately upon your employment and will indoctrinate you in the particular duties of that company and that apartment house?

Property management is not a young industry. It has grown tremendously in the past twenty-five years; it still has few legal hedges placed around it. Any corporation or company has all the legal rights of an individual, though it has few of the legal liabilities or responsibilities. Among other things, the courts of our land have decreed that a corporation can be held liable for trespass, negligence, nuisance, assault and battery, false imprisonment, malicious prosecution, libel and slander. A fourteenth-century court in England said that corporations could not be held to some of the foregoing responsibilities, "nor can they commit treason, or be outlaws or excommunicated, for they have no souls." However, the people who make and comprise corporations are assumed to have had "souls" at one time. The resident managers, then, can perhaps help the corporate bodies to find them again.

ABOUT THE AUTHOR

M. M. "Steemy" Holt is now retired after 35 years of owning and managing her own businesses and rental properties. She was raised in Oklahoma City, Oklahoma and came to Washington State in 1946. She now lives in the Seattle area in Washington State.

Mrs. Holt writes: "While working with resident managers, I became alarmed with their lack of guidance and training. They seemed hungry for information concerning their field. After extensive research I found the situation has not changed much in the last 30 years. This book is in response to that need"

www.ingramcontent.com/pod-product-compliance
Lightning Source LLC
Chambersburg PA
CBHW051447280526
45785CB00003B/1462